100 THINGS LIONS FANS SHOULD KNOW & DO BEFORE THEY DIE

Paula Pasche

TRIUMPH
BOOKS

Library of Congress Cataloging-in-Publication Data

Pasche, Paula, 1955–
    100 things Lions fans should know & do before they die / Paula Pasche.
    p. cm.
    Includes bibliographical references.
    ISBN 978-1-60078-729-4 (pbk.)
    1. Detroit Lions (Football team)—History. 2.   Detroit Lions (Football team)—Miscellanea. I. Title. II. Title: One hundred things Lion fans should know & do before they die.
    GV956.D4.P34 2012
    796.332'640977434—dc23
                                        2012019598

This book is available in quantity at special discounts for your group or organization. For further information, contact:

Triumph Books LLC
814 North Franklin Street
Chicago, Illinois 60610
(312) 337-0747
www.triumphbooks.com

Printed in U.S.A.
ISBN: 978-1-60078-729-4
Design by Patricia Frey
Photos courtesy of AP Images unless otherwise indicated

To my dad, who took me to my first Lions game,
and to all Lions fans everywhere

Contents

Acknowledgments. ix

Introduction. xi

1 Barry Sanders, Face of the Franchise 1

2 The Lions' Diehard Fans. 5

3 Megatron Always a Threat. 8

4 Worst NFL Season Ever 10

5 Quietly Mayhew Works His Magic. 12

6 It Is the Motor City. 15

7 Road Losers No More 17

8 Fords Keep an Eye on Team 19

9 A Detroit Tradition. 22

10 1935 Championship, A First. 24

11 Old, Bald, and Still Kicking. 27

12 They Call Him "The Franchise" 30

13 The Smell of Success 34

14 The Blond Bomber 36

15 Another NFL Championship. 39

16 Scott Mitchell's Ups and Downs 41

17 Time for a Turn-Around. 43

18 One Playoff Win in 54 Years. 46

19 At Last Back to the Playoffs. 48

20 One Loss, Multiple Changes 50

21 Forget the Millen Era 52

22 Joey Not a Favorite 55

23 Biggest Draft Bust. 57

24 Russ Thomas Made His Mark 59

25 Suh Does The Stomp 61

26 Five Starters in 44 Days 63

27 Are You Ready for *Monday Night Football*? 65

28 Mike Utley Full of Life 68

29 Fontes, A Man With a Smile 70

30 Moore a Fan Favorite 72

31 Best Seventh-Round Pick Ever? 76

32 Sims Hot From the Start 78

33 Back-to-Back Titles 82

34 Out on a Winning Note 84

35 Built with Character 86

36 Gridiron Heroes 89

37 Emotions Rule the Day 91

38 Disheartened Ross Leaves 93

39 The Day the Music Died 95

40 From Portsmouth to Detroit 98

41 RIP Chuck Hughes 99

42 Tiger Stadium, A Longtime Home 102

43 Add This to Your Bucket List 104

44 No Happy Ending 106

45 Once a Fan, Now President 107

46 Monte Clark's Two Stints 110

47 Don't Forget Mongo or Karras 112

48 The Calvin Rule 114

49 Creekmur's Wait Pays Off 116

50 Best Free Agent Signing Ever? 119

51 Another One Bites the Dust 121

52 Jim Schwartz to the Rescue 123

53 He Took the Wind 125

54 Reggie Rogers Kills Three 128

55 Lem Barney 130

56 One Fearsome Dude 133

57 Detroit Lions Academy 136

58 Football Times Two 138

59 Tailgate Haven 140

60 Third Title in Six Years 142

61 Life Before Hanson 145

62 Loud and Proud 148

63 A Pair of Heisman Quarterbacks 150

64 Landry a Standout 152

65 Mel Gray Puts On a Show 154

66 Spielman a Throwback 156

67 Dick "Night Train" Lane 159

68 Green Bay Sent Packing 161

69 Playoff Highs and Lows 165

70 Plimpton's Folly 169

71 Breaking the Vikings' Curse 171

72 Location is Everything 175

73 Famous Detroiters Big Fans 177

74 Playoffs Worth the Wait 179

75 Detroit Winner at Super Bowl XL 181

76 Another Detroit Tradition 183

77 Totally Multidimensional 185

78 Father and Son Lions 187

79 The Old Ball Games 189

80 Gary Danielson's Ups and Downs. 190

81 All-You-Can-Eat Seats. 193

82 RIP Tom "Killer" Kowalski. 195

83 25 Years of Brandstatter 198

84 History Comes Alive. 202

85 Angry Man March. 205

86 Andolsek Gone Too Soon. 207

87 Morton's Impact. 209

88 Porcher, A Community Man 212

89 Visit Training Camp, Learn New Words 214

90 First Impressions. 216

91 From Player to Player Personnel 220

92 Pro Football Hall of Fame. 221

93 The Handshake. 223

94 Celebrate in Greektown 227

95 Working the Line 228

96 Detroit Lions Charities 231

97 Coney Wars. 233

98 History at the Lions' Expense 235

99 Bears-Lions Rivalry 237

100 God Bless YouTube 239

Sources 242

Acknowledgments

When my family first moved to Detroit in 1969, my dad took me to Tiger Stadium to watch a Lions game. It was my dad who taught me football, patiently answering all my questions while watching games on television. Seeing an NFL game in person for the first time was such an eye-opener. I was hooked and even as a kid, I thought television just didn't do the game justice. Tiger Stadium was a great place to watch the Lions, mostly because we were lucky enough to sit in box seats and not behind a post. We went to several games that season, including Thanksgiving. I understand the economics of building enclosed stadiums, but watching football outdoors is the ultimate experience. Ask anyone in Green Bay.

At that point I never would have thought I'd be writing a book about the Lions. Actually at that point in my life, I had no idea that I would become a sportswriter.

My dad died while I was writing this book, but I know he's watching me and had a hand on my shoulder while I was writing.

It's been a fascinating ride, looking back at the times in the 1950s when the Lions had the makings of a dynasty, winning three NFL championships in six seasons. Digging back through the Lions' history for these pages would not have been possible without the use of the clip books in the Lions library. They have books of newspaper clippings back to the 1930s. I couldn't have written the book without the newspaper accounts from the *Detroit Free Press*, *Detroit News*, *The Oakland Press*, and *Booth Newspapers*. I also picked up information from old stories on the Internet.

As a sportswriter for *The Oakland Press*, I covered the Lions in the 1990s and again have been back on the beat since 2009. As I started writing, many of the memories started flooding back. Is it a coincidence that the Lions' turnaround started when I got back on the beat? Absolutely.

For statistics I depended on Pro-Football-Reference.com.

Thanks to Lions president Tom Lewand for taking the time to sit down with me to fill in historical gaps and also look to the future.

Thanks to the Lions media relations department, in particular Bill Keenist, senior vice president of communications. And a special nod to media relations interns Kait Sawyer and Andrew Mouranic who were huge on encouragement and helping me dig through the shelves of dusty old clip books.

All of my friends pushed and encouraged me throughout the process, but a few were stand-outs, including Jennifer Hammond, John Kreger, Annemarie Schiavi Pedersen, Angelique Chengelis, and John Torchetti.

My friend Tom Kowalski died two months before I signed the contract. He was also a mentor who was starting his 30th season of covering the team. I used information from a few of his clips, but I would have loved to pick his brain. I did my best to make him proud.

I could have never written this book without support from my family. A huge thanks and a big hug.

Introduction

Detroit may be the Motor City, but a close look under the hood reveals that, besides automobiles, it's a city driven by sports lovers. Hockeytown? Sure. But that's only because the Red Wings won four Stanley Cup championships in a dozen years (1997, 1998, 2002, and 2008).

The fans love their Detroit Tigers (World Series champions in 1968 and 1984) and Pistons (NBA championships in 1989, 1990, and 2004), as well as University of Michigan football and Michigan State basketball.

Everyone knows—and former Red Wings grinder Darren McCarty once said it out loud—that when the Lions win a Super Bowl it will become very clear that Detroit is a football town. The town will explode, in a good way.

The day is getting closer.

While the Lions are one of a handful of NFL teams that have never even played in a Super Bowl, these days you are not looked upon as a lunatic if you say out loud that day is not too far away. Quarterback Matthew Stafford, wide receiver Calvin Johnson, and defensive tackle Ndamukong Suh form the nucleus of a club that shot up to 10–6 in 2011 just three years separated from 0–16. Or as many Lions fans call it, "Oh and 16."

The misguided ways of Matt Millen have faded into the distant past. It's a good time to be a Detroit Lions fan. Finally.

Even through all the losing and disappointment, the questionable drafts and bad coaching moves, the fans have stood by their beloved Lions. So when ranking what is so special about the Lions from 1 to 100 it's clear that the fans must rank near the top. I gave them the No. 2 spot. And, in reality, it wasn't that tough of a decision. That is not a slap to the fans, but a credit to No. 1.

When I think Lions, and I don't believe I'm alone, one face, one number, one rumbling-tumbling running back stands out. While he hasn't played since 1998, Barry Sanders is in many ways still the face of the Lions. He didn't bring a championship to town, but it's not because he didn't try. Sanders gave the Lions respectability. He made the offense a threat each time it took the field. He made each game special, each season full of endless possibilities. Debate among yourselves, but Barry Sanders is tops in my book, which just happens to be this book.

I was fortunate to cover the Lions as a sportswriter through many of Barry Sanders' seasons. Those games will always stand out as a highlight of my career. When doing research for this book, I went to YouTube to watch Sanders' highlights and had trouble tearing myself away. He was spectacular.

Speaking of spectacular, while it's still early in Calvin Johnson's career, we've seen enough from the wide receiver known as Megatron to give him the No. 3 spot. As the Lions have started to win, Johnson is also getting more well-deserved recognition around the league. It culminated in the spring of 2012 when he was voted to the cover of the Madden NFL 13 video game. A big deal, damn the curse.

It wasn't so easy to rank Nos. 4 through 100, especially while trying to give history its due and also paying proper respect to more recent history from the 1980s and 1990s.

Among the most enjoyable—yet dirty and dusty—tasks was to dig through history, looking through the bound newspaper clippings dating back to the 1930s. The pages were brittle to the touch, yellow, and chock full of history. Fascinating.

While the Lions have not won a Super Bowl, they have won four NFL championships, the last one in 1957. The logo was much the same then as now, although the pay was, shall we say, a bit less.

Couldn't forget the legends, the Hall of Famers who wore the uniform—some I'd heard of and others I hadn't. Joe Schmidt, Yale

Lary, Lem Barney, Dick "Night Train" Layne, and Charlie Sanders each are deserving of their own book.

A great peek behind the scenes of the Lions in the 1960s came through reading George Plimpton's *Paper Lion*, which was first published in 1966. I can't say enough about the book. Plimpton's writing is lyrical. Better yet, while he joined the team for training camp one summer, he was able to open the doors to the locker room and the dorm rooms. The premise of the book is having Plimpton try to play quarterback in a preseason game, but it is so much more than that. It was riveting and opened my eyes to some of the Lions' greats of the past like Alex Karras, Wayne Walker, Milt Plum, and Joe Schmidt.

It was a bit easier to write this book because I had witnessed several Lions games at Tiger Stadium as a kid with my dad. I had covered several more games at the Silverdome as a young sportswriter, learning the ins and out of the NFL. Then it was on to Ford Field, a Detroit gem.

As a reporter I've sweated on the sideline through hot, humid training camps from Saginaw to Allen Park. There's nothing quite like seeing an NFL team come together from draft day through camp and during the season. The only thing better was delving into history and trying to capture the spirit of a team that was first brought to Detroit in 1934.

In listing the highlights and lowlights of the Lions and the city of Detroit, I did my best. However, it's certainly not a closed subject. Let's look at it as a conversation starter.

Read and enjoy.

1 Barry Sanders, Face of the Franchise

The 1996 season had been dreadful. It was Wayne Fontes' last, and there was one game remaining—on Monday night in San Francisco. The Lions were flying out from Detroit on Saturday. With a 5–10 record, most players were just going through the motions at practice that Friday.

After practice, Bill Keenist, who was in charge of media relations, went on a search for Barry Sanders who would be named All-Pro the next morning. A national reporter wanted a few comments from Sanders, and Keenist chased down Sanders for the interview.

By the time Keenist arrived at the locker room at the Silverdome, it was empty. But Sanders' clothes were still hanging in his stall, a sign he was somewhere in the building. Keenist looked in the obvious places and then by chance went into the weight room. Only one player was lifting, and it was Barry Sanders.

The running back said he had about 30 minutes left and then would be happy to comply with a few comments. So Keenist left, but when he went back the weight room was dark, the locker room was still empty, and Sanders' clothes still hung in his stall. On a lark, Keenist went down to the field. It was a dreary December, so it was fairly dark on the Silverdome field, but the safety lights provided a bit of illumination.

One player was on the field running sprints. Of course it was Barry Sanders. It should have been no surprise, but it was the end of the season and still Sanders was working hard. Barry Sanders was great because of his on-field, head-spinning, jaw-dropping moves. They didn't happen by accident. Greatness is often achieved in weight rooms and practice fields when no one is watching.

Barry Sanders heads into the end zone against the Chicago Bears for a first-quarter touchdown on Sunday, November 24, 1996, in Chicago. Sanders became the first NFL player to run for 1,000 yards in eight consecutive seasons.
(AP Photo/Michael S. Green)

In that game at San Francisco—a 24–14 loss—Sanders carried the ball 28 times for 175 yards and a touchdown.

Sanders set the standard for hard work throughout his 10 seasons with the Lions, a team that had drafted him with the third overall pick at the urging of Coach Wayne Fontes who wanted Barry over another Sanders who was available, Deion.

It almost seems hard to believe now, but prior to the draft there were concerns about his size. Sanders is 5'8", but he was not a small running back. His playing weight was 203, and he carried much of his weight in his thick muscular legs, giving him a low center of gravity.

He won the 1988 Heisman Trophy after shattering records in his three seasons at Oklahoma State. In that season he averaged 7.6 yards a carry and more than 200 yards per game, including four games of more than 300 yards.

The question was: would it translate to the NFL?

Sanders had no trouble making the adjustment. He had worn No. 21 in college but was offered No. 20, the same number worn by former Lions' greats Lem Barney and Billy Sims.

It was clear starting in his rookie season that records or individual accomplishments were not Sanders' goal. In his first season he finished second in rushing yards and could have been first, but he declined to go back into the final game to pick up 10 yards.

Never flashy, when Sanders scored a touchdown—he scored 109 in his career—he would hand the ball back to the official like he'd been there before. He didn't spend money on clothes—his teammates would gently chide him for his fashion choices. One time a carload of local sportswriters were heading into the Silverdome parking lot a few hours before game time and were cut off by a guy in an old blue sedan. It was Sanders.

Sanders was worth the price of admission to every game. He could break through a defense and find space where no one else could. He was tough to tackle, and at times he could embarrass defenses.

Barry Sanders' Best Five Games

The Hall of Fame running back posted three career games of 200 yards or more. Here are his top five rushing yard games:

1. 237 yards, 26 attempts—November 13, 1994.
2. 220 yards, 23 attempts—November 24, 1991.
3. 216 yards, 24 attempts—November 23, 1997.
4. 215 yards, 24 attempts—October 12, 1997.
5. 194 yards, 40 attempts—September 19, 1994.

The Lions made it to the playoffs during five of Sanders' 10 seasons. His greatest season was in 1997 when he topped the 2,000-yard mark for the first and only time. In his final season he rushed for 1,491 yards, ending his four-year streak of running for more than 1,500 yards.

Sports Illustrated's Paul Zimmerman once wrote of Sanders, "It doesn't matter where the play is blocked; he'll find his own soft spot.... The scheme doesn't matter with Sanders. He can run from any alignment. While other people are stuck with joints, he seems to have ball bearings in his legs that give him a mechanical advantage.... Sanders' finest runs often occur when he takes the handoff and, with a couple of moves, turns the line of scrimmage into a broken field.... Nobody has ever created such turmoil at the point of attack as Sanders has.... Knock on wood, he seems indestructible."

Weeks before the end of what would be his final season, I wrote a story asking if fans, writers, and coaches had come to take Barry Sanders for granted. At the time he didn't even know how many years he had left on his contract.

Sanders unexpectedly quit football days before training camp for the 1999 season. (See No. 39, page 95). Some fans were angry with their hero. Time, however, has healed most wounds.

Sanders married a local television anchor, Lauren Campbell. Together they have three children and reside in suburban Detroit.

When he was not much more than a toddler, Sanders' oldest son, Barry James, would occasionally attend practice at the Silverdome. He looked just like his dad and would get excited to see his dad score a touchdown in practice. It wasn't apparent then, but the son got some of his dad's running back genes. He has committed to play running back at Stanford in 2012.

All these years later, Barry Sanders is still the face of the organization. That could eventually change with the current bunch, but he is still the guy. Barry Sanders still brings back the warmest and fuzziest memories of the Lions.

No one has forgotten how he could run with a football. He was magical.

2 The Lions' Diehard Fans

Diehard. Proud. Passionate. Resilient. Eternally optimistic.

Those six words might best describe Detroit Lions fans who have had their hearts broken and dreams dumped on, perhaps more consistently than the fans of any other NFL team.

Still they cheer.

As one fan summed up the past 30 or so years, "Mike Utley, Eric Andolsek, Charles Rogers' two collarbones, Matthew Stafford's shoulder, Barry Sanders' retirement. Only the Lions. Worst part of fandom! I mean seriously...who gets hit by a truck mowing their lawn? This is crap that only happens to the Lions."

Andolsek, the starting left guard, was killed while weed whacking around the mailbox of his home in Louisiana in June 1992. Utley was paralyzed after a freak on-field play seven months prior. Charles Rogers, a first-round draft pick, was a total bust after breaking his collarbone two years in a row. Sanders retired the day before training camp in 1999.

Then there's the epic, NFL record 0–16 season in 2008. That did send a few fans to the ledge, but most stayed. After all, they could only improve. There is nothing worse than suffering through a season without a single win. Is there?

If the Lions fans can live through all of that, they can face anything. Now that the team is showing signs of a turn-around, the fans are being rewarded with wins. That's all they want, a team that can compete every Sunday and an occasional Monday.

The coaches and players haven't lived through it all like the fans have, but they understand they are lucky to play in a city with such passionate fans. When the Lions clinched a playoff spot with a win over the Chargers on December 24, 2011, Coach Jim Schwartz led the players around the edge of Ford Field for a victory lap where they high-fived the fans and thanked them for their support.

"This town loves a winner, and when things are going well you get a lot of fans and they are real fans, they're not part of that hardcore goup at the center, they're real fans not casual fly-by-night fans, they really care," Lions president Tom Lewand said.

"That's what you see in this area—same thing with the Tigers, same thing with the Red Wings. When things are going well, it's real pride, it's not just bandwagon jumping. There's a real pride in our own product of Detroit doing well," Lewand added.

He uses Kid Rock, who is from Detroit, as an example. Even if people don't like his music, they are Kid Rock fans because they see him as one of Detroit's own who has done well.

"It's why even when we compete with each other, it's a little like the inter-family squabble. I can smack my brother around, but no one else can. That's the approach we've taken historically here. Those of us who are loyal to Ford Motor Company can take shots at General Motors and Chrysler, but once the Japanese start rolling into town, look out," Lewand said. "That's been the case forever, we have a fierce sense of loyalty and a fierce sense of pride in our community. I think sports in general and the Lions in particular embody those characteristics."

Even though Detroit has earned the moniker of Hockeytown because of the Red Wings' success, everyone in town knows Detroit is a football city. If the Lions ever win big and make it to the Super Bowl, this town might just explode with pride.

With the success at the end of 2010 (6–10) and throughout 2011 (10–6 and a trip to the playoffs), the fans are responding. Even though the jobless rate is incredibly high, the Lions sold out every game in 2011 and all but one in 2010.

"I'm not sure there's any other team in town that could have weathered the extended drought we had as well as we did, that's completely because of the support of our fans. As great as the fan base the Red Wings and Tigers have and even the Pistons, it's still not what we have. You can still be in a position to sell out some games when you're 0–16. There are teams in this league that are playoff teams and they can't sell out," Lewand said, using the Cincinnati Bengals as an example. They sold out just two of eight games in 2011.

The Lions are well aware that their fans don't respond to empty rhetoric. They don't want fancy slogans.

"They don't respond well to sales pitches and fancy perfume on the pig, they want the real deal," Lewand said. "They're smart—they see it, they know, you can't fool these people."

All they want is a winner. They've paid their dues, and they are ready for the payoff.

3 Megatron Always a Threat

They call him Megatron. He's a specimen—6'5" and 236 well-sculpted pounds. Calvin Johnson, the Lions wide receiver, possesses a 45" vertical leap and mitts that were made to catch footballs. He's humble to a fault. When he smiles, his whole face lights up. And he smiles when he catches passes, especially touchdowns.

It was the fourth game in the 2011 season in the glitzy football palace known as Cowboys Stadium. The Lions were threatening, ,and Calvin Johnson saw something in the defense he thought he could exploit. So he caught the eye of quarterback Matthew Stafford and pointed to the roof.

The Dallas defense didn't catch the little hand signal. Stafford saw it and knew that Johnson wanted it thrown high so he could leap above the triple coverage.

"I don't [signal] all the time, if I'm definitely feeling it, yeah, there's been a couple times," Johnson said with a big smile, of course.

He and Stafford can almost read each other's minds. They could become the top quarterback-receiver combination in the NFL. Stafford would love that.

"You'd want to be known as that," Stafford said. "It's not something [where] I'm going to force-feed him the ball. When he gets a good look and gets open, I'm going to try to hit him every time."

When a team mistakenly leaves Johnson in single coverage, they are likely to pay.

Johnson got off to the hottest of starts in 2011 when he caught eight touchdown passes in the first four games, all wins. Still, that didn't impress former NFL receiver Cris Carter, who didn't rank Johnson in his top five NFL receivers early in 2011.

Possibly Johnson's biggest fan, Nate Burleson, sits a few lockers away. While Johnson said he wasn't bothered by Carter's comments, Burleson took offense. "I feel like right now Calvin Johnson is definitely in the top five and arguably the best receiver in the game—at his height, his strength, his ability to jump, there aren't too many receivers that can do what he does, period," Burleson said. "His speed is incredible, he jumps a 45" vertical, he has huge hands, he can bench press 225, as much as linebackers."

Carter also said there was no need to double-team Johnson. Burleson would love for opposing defensive coordinators to take that advice. "If you single-cover Calvin Johnson, I guarantee we'll win nine times out of 10," Burleson said.

Johnson, in his fifth season with the Lions, finally made it to the playoffs in 2011. He was all of that right from the get-go. Johnson hauled in a team-high 12 receptions and set a wild-card record with 211 receiving yards in the loss at New Orleans. He also had a pair of touchdown catches. A month earlier when the Lions lost to the Saints, Johnson had been held to 69 yards.

Big game, big-play C.J. In the final two games, Johnson had 455 receiving yards. He set a personal best with 244 receiving yards at Green Bay in the regular season finale.

Johnson finished the 2011 season (including playoffs) with 1,892 yards, 18 touchdowns, 108 receptions, and an invitation to the Pro Bowl. Those first two stats smashed the Lions' franchise

Calvin's Best Games

Calvin Johnson's fifth season was his best so far with the Lions. Here are his top five career games based on yardage.
1. January 1, 2012—244 yards, 11 catches, 1 TD
2. December 18, 2011—214 yards, 9 catches 2 TDs
3. November 22, 2009—161 yards, 7 catches, 1 TD
4. October 19, 2008—154 yards, 2 catches, 1 TD
5. December 19, 2010—152 yards, 10 catches, 0 TD

records, and he's tied for second with Brett Perriman for receptions. Herman Moore had 123 in 1995.

It's not surprising that Johnson, a quiet guy off the field, is not too flashy when he scores touchdowns by the pair. In fact, he's developed a habit of spiking the football into the wall behind the end zone. It's no dance, but it's totally Calvin Johnson.

"I think it was excitement, the energy, and basically telling everybody, 'You can't stop me.' I didn't talk to him about it, I was trying to give him some room because he had rage in his eyes at that moment that I wanted no part of," Burleson said, referring to a touchdown against the Cowboys.

Johnson, the second overall pick in the 2007 draft, got a fast start with the Lions, winning six of his first eight games in his rookie season. In the next three seasons, the Lions won a total of eight games. If you're looking for a reason that Johnson might be one of the NFL's biggest secrets, that is it. There is no spotlight when you play on a losing team.

He made it to the cover of *Sports Illustrated* in 2011. He's literally a human highlight reel every Sunday night. The secret is out.

Worst NFL Season Ever

0–16.

It was more of a nightmare season than any fans of any NFL team had ever survived. You know how they say that even a blind squirrel occasionally finds a nut? There were no nuts for the Lions that season. It was 2008. The Lions started with a 34–21 loss at Atlanta and ended with a 31–21 shellacking at Green Bay's Lambeau Field.

0–16.

Eight of the losses were by 10 points or less. The closest the Lions came to winning was a 12–10 loss to the Vikings at the Metrodome on October 12.

Detroit's starting quarterback duties were spread between Dan Orlovsky (seven games), Daunte Culpepper (five games), and Jon Kitna (four games). It didn't matter. None of them could power the offense enough to grab a win.

It was the end of the road for Coach Rod Marinelli, who was 10–38 in three seasons. The embarrassment was also enough for owner William Clay Ford to finally fire General Manager Matt Millen, who had built the 2008 squad. Millen had accomplished something no other general manager had—the worst eight-year record in the history of the modern NFL (31–97). He was let go on September 24, 2008, but the damage had already been done. Not even a miracle worker can completely rebuild a team starting in late September.

0–16.

It all ended on Lambeau Field on December 28. The Packers had lost five straight entering the game and certainly didn't want to be the only team that couldn't beat the lowly Lions that season. Quarterback Aaron Rodgers was his usual spectacular self, completing 21-of-31 passes for 308 yards with three touchdowns and no interceptions. He could have been better, but his receivers dropped a half-dozen passes.

Two running backs—Ryan Grant and DeShawn Wynn—passed the 100-yard mark and two receivers—Greg Jennings and Donald Driver—caught passes for more than 100 yards apiece.

Still, the Lions fought the hard fight. The Lions battled back to knot it at 14–14 late in the third quarter, but then they were outscored by 17–7 in the final 15 minutes.

Running back Kevin Smith, who was in his rookie season, accumulated 976 yards and the wisdom of a veteran that season.

He told reporters after that final loss that he was keeping the gloves as a reminder of how horrid it was to be the NFL's laughingstock.

He ran for 92 yards that day but was also whistled for a costly 15-yard unsportsmanlike conduct penalty after jawing with cornerback Tramon Williams who had pushed him out of bounds. Bad penalties were just one of the issues for that season and that day.

Orlovsky said they were totally embarrassed. They had tried, but they just didn't do enough.

After that game, Marinelli said the record spoke for itself and they had no one to blame but themselves—coachspeak at the highest or lowest level. To his credit, the Lions didn't give up that day. They didn't blame the brutal cold, they just didn't play well enough to win. The Cheesehead fans chanted, "0 and 16" in the waning minutes as if the Lions really needed to hear it.

The team became the NFL's new benchmark for badness, over-taking the expansion Tampa Bay Bucs who went winless (0–14) in 1976. The 2008 Lions had been perfect in the preseason but were outscored 517–268 when it counted.

The long-suffering Lions fans persevered with two thoughts in mind: It couldn't get worse, and at least Matt Millen was gone.

5 Quietly Mayhew Works His Magic

Martin Mayhew possesses a quiet strength. As an NFL cornerback, he once finished a game with a broken arm. At just 5'8" and 172 pounds, he played 118 NFL regular season games during eight seasons. Mayhew was a starter for the Washington Redskins in Super Bowl XXVI.

After finishing his NFL stint, he attended law school at Georgetown. Mayhew was promoted to Lions' general manager on December 29, 2008, following the record-setting 0–16 season and the subsequent dismissal of Matt Millen.

Mayhew has repeatedly said—and it's been repeated by team President Tom Lewand and Coach Jim Schwartz—that they were not building a team for the short run. They were working on building a championship team that will rank among the NFL's elite (the New England Patriots, for example) for years to come.

Mayhew chose Jim Schwartz, a first-time NFL coach, and along with Lewand, the three marched forward. For the first time in many seasons, all three were on the same page.

Mayhew's first official move was trading wide receiver Roy Williams and a seventh-round pick to Dallas for first-, third-, and sixth-round picks in 2009. After all, Millen's poor drafts had left the Lions' cupboards bare.

His first draft pick with the top overall pick in 2009 was quarterback Matthew Stafford. It seemed almost like a no-brainer, but there have been busts high in the draft, and Mayhew and his team had to make sure Stafford was the guy. Expectations ran high, and after two injury-riddled seasons, Stafford proved Mayhew right in his first complete season in 2011, shattering most franchise passing records.

Under Mayhew the first season was ugly. The Lions rebounded from 0–16 with a 2–14 record. Clearly, Mayhew would have liked a faster start, but he had a plan and stuck with it—quietly.

Mayhew, a friendly sort, will say hello and precious little else to the Detroit media as he heads out onto the field each day for training camp and outdoor practices. It's just that he has nothing to say. He traditionally meets with the Lions beat writers for breakfast on the morning of the second day of the NFL Combine. It gives them a little insight into what he's thinking.

Very organized, Mayhew has a draft strategy. He and his staff can't watch enough film. Once they write out their draft board—how they see the picks going—they just watch more film. He obviously has no interest in the spotlight, he doesn't want to explain his moves, he just wants to create a winning tradition in Detroit.

In 2010, his second full season as GM, Mayhew and the Lions made progress. They drafted defensive tackle Ndamukong Suh with the second overall pick.

By this time the roster had been almost completely redone. He knew he'd have a tough time drawing free agents to a losing club, so he traded for starters like Corey Williams, Chris Houston, Shaun Hill, Rob Sims, and Tony Scheffler. He attracted free agents Kyle Vanden Bosch and Nate Burleson because they had worked with Jim Schwartz and offensive coordinator Scott Linehan, respectively.

Stafford was injured, and the secondary changed from game to game due to injuries. But still the Lions were able to win their final four games and finish 6–10.

In 2011 everyone started to see what Mayhew was all about. His Lions went 10–6 in the regular season and made their first trip to the playoffs since the 1999 season. They lost in the wild-card playoff game at New Orleans. Their goal wasn't to get to the playoffs, however, it was to win in the postseason. They came up short, but it was quite a turn-around from 0–16 to 10–6 in three short years.

That tells you all you need to know about Martin Mayhew.

6 It Is the Motor City

If your chest swelled up with a little Motor City pride when those Chrysler commercials with Eminem first appeared in 2011, you might want to get a closer look at the reason we are a city. Take a tour of the Ford Rouge facility, in particular the Dearborn Truck Plant, and get a look at how the vehicles you see on the road are built. In this case, it's the Ford F-150 Truck.

You've seen the photos from the plants, but I must admit it was still amazing to see it in person. After spending a few hours on the tour—it's self-guided so you can take it at your own pace—I may never look at a Ford F-150 the same way again. Self-guided doesn't mean you walk in the door to the visitor's center and fend for yourself. There are guides all over, including when you first get off the bus that delivers you from The Henry Ford Museum a few miles away.

If you have any questions, the guides have the answers.

The tour is broken into five parts, including two movies that are each about 13 minutes long. The first is in the Legacy Theater and runs every 20 minutes. It focuses on the history of the plant, but it's not boring because they have rare film clips of Henry Ford and even shots of the early plants. And to their credit, they talk about the unions getting involved with the plants and mention that Henry Ford wanted nothing to do with them at first. So it wasn't all sappy public relations drivel. It was the real deal.

Across the hall is the Art of Manufacturing theater in which all the seats swivel 360 degrees for the multimedia presentation on seven screens. It shows a vehicle being built from what was once a hunk of steel. There were scenes where the floor vibrated and when wind machines were used, and the host said there was smell-o-vision, too. The film was just 13 minutes long. The music was created just for these movies and performed by the Detroit Symphony Orchestra. It was spectacular.

From there it was up the elevator to the observation deck to get a better idea of the spread of the plant that covers territory one mile long and three-quarters of a mile wide. The truck plant I'd be seeing next was built with a green roof (to help insulate the facility) and skylights (to provide light when available). It was snowy the day I was there, but there were displays in the observation tower showing how growing sedum (a ground cover) on the roof helps insulate the building. It was a clear day so you could see the downtown Detroit skyline, including the Renaissance Center. It's all pretty fascinating stuff, really.

The actual plant tour lets you walk on an elevated walkway above the assembly line. There are video stations, signs, and helpful guides wearing orange shirts along the way.

I was amazed watching the truck boxes hook up with the cabs. To each his own I guess, but I found it fascinating how the red boxes automatically were attached to red cabs and so on. Also something interesting to me was that the bodies come to the assembly plant after the final painting process. Then they take the doors off—to make it easier for work to be done on the interiors. Putting the doors back on is one of the final steps.

This plant was immaculate and the aisles were twice as wide as older plants, at least that's what one guide told me. For every shift there are 1,000 workers. They must each do a different job at least once a week so they don't get bored. Each worker has a minute to complete his or her part of the process in the plant, which produces 60 Ford F-150s per hour. The tour gives you an ideal viewpoint from above.

Even though I've lived in Detroit since my high school days, the only time I'd visited an auto plant was when I was much younger and my Dad, who worked for Oldsmobile, took our family to a plant tour in Lansing. I won't say how long ago that was, but it was before robots. Obviously before the Rouge tour I was aware robotics play a large role in building cars, but there are many parts that can only be handled by humans, which is a good thing.

The tour ends with a look around the Legacy Gallery that features a vintage Thunderbird and the 20 millionth Ford built.

You can take the tour in any order, but I went 1 through 5 because it gave me the best chance to see the assembly line after their 30-minute lunch break. They can't guarantee the assembly line will be moving every day, it depends on truck orders, time of year, and other considerations. So a call ahead might be a wise idea if you want to see the assembly line in action.

The tours are run out of The Henry Ford Museum. Buy your ticket there, then hop on one of the buses that depart every 20 minutes. It's about a 10-minute ride (you'll go past the Lions practice facility) to the plant.

These are not the best days in Detroit, but the auto manufacturers seem to be rising out of the ashes. Building cars is part of the heritage in Detroit, and taking a plant tour is a good way to celebrate just that.

7 Road Losers No More

They say it's tough to win on the road in the NFL. Never has a team offered more proof of that than the Detroit Lions.

They played 26 road games during parts of four seasons (2007–10) and lost every single one consecutively, setting an NFL record. It's not the kind of record the Lions will share with their grandchildren, though.

In the unlikeliest of scenarios, the team's fortunes changed. With a 23–20 OT win in Tampa on December 19, 2010, the Lions could finally quit answering questions about the god-awful streak.

"When that streak is talked about and all of that, a lot of these players and coaches don't know what you're talking about, they haven't been a part of it. It's kind of not right to say they are a part of it," left tackle Jeff Backus said. "Dom [Raiola] and I and a few other guys have been here the whole time. It's nice to get the monkey off our back, and hopefully that's the last streak that we have and we can start some positive ones and get this thing turned around."

It was not the perfect setup. Drew Stanton, the third-string quarterback, was in as a starter with Matthew Stafford and Shaun Hill injured. Dave Rayner was kicking for the injured Jason Hanson.

Until that balmy afternoon in Tampa, the Lions had won just three games in the season.

With 1:39 left on the clock and the Bucs up 20–17, Stanton started the fourth-quarter drive on Detroit's own 32. Stanton was 4-of-8 with key passes to Calvin Johnson for 23 yards on a second-and-6, a 19-yard pass to Bryant Johnson on second-and-10, and a 12-yarder to Tony Scheffler on a third-and-10.

Then Rayner, who grew up in the Detroit suburbs as a Lions fan, stepped in and kicked a 28-yard field goal to tie the game with no time left.

After winning the toss, the Lions started on their own 21 with a 26-yard run by Maurice Morris, followed by a 14-yard scamper by Jahvid Best.

On a third-and-8 at Tampa's 37, Stanton threw to Calvin Johnson, who ran out of bounds at the Tampa 25 after a 12-yard gain.

Stanton never saw Johnson make the catch that secured the win. "I knew they were going to bring an internal blitz, so I have to sit in here and take this one and trust he's going to get to his spot. I still haven't seen it. I'm sure he made an unbelievable catch,"

Stanton said immediately after the game. He was 23-of-37 for 252 yards, one touchdown, and no interceptions.

Rayner stepped in and kicked a 34-yard field goal to win the game.

It was the second straight win for Stanton whose blood runs ice-cold, the perfect temperature for an NFL quarterback.

"Drew is calm. Drew's a gunslinger. He's been in tough games, he's played in tough games before. He was ice cold out there, it showed," left guard Rob Sims said. "It was like, 'Let's march down the field, get this field goal, and get out of here.' That was the way we were thinking. I'll go to war with Drew any day."

It was a big day for Stanton but an even bigger win for the franchise.

"Winning on the road is a step we needed to take. I can't help but think this is a game that maybe we don't win early in the season," coach Jim Schwartz said. "We're becoming a battle-hardened team. This is a franchise that hadn't been used to playing a lot of close games, and this year we have."

It was the start of four straight wins to end the season.

Indeed the Lions had started another road streak. They finished 2010 with two straight road wins and began 2011 with four consecutive road wins before losing in Chicago.

When looking for turn-around points for the Lions, this win is a good start.

8 Fords Keep an Eye on Team

There's always a clear sign that owner William Clay Ford Sr. is going to be present at Lions' practice. His golf cart, designed like a Mustang and painted royal blue, is taken out from the garage. It even has turn signals. Sometimes he drives himself out to the field, while other times he is chauffeured.

Ford, the Lions owner and chairman who is also the director emeritus of the Ford Motor Company board of directors, likes to keep an eye on his guys. Ford bought the Lions in November 1963 for $4.5 million and officially took over the club on January 10, 1964.

His interest in the team grew from when his father, Edsel Ford, took him to see the Lions at the University of Detroit Stadium in 1934, their first season in Detroit. Prior to purchasing the franchise, he had been a club director in 1956 and was asked by then Lions president Edwin J. "Andy" Anderson to become the Lions president in 1961.

The 2011 season was his 48th as owner. Along the way Ford has been intensely loyal to the coaches and general managers that he's hired to run the team. Even though fans were ready to see Matt Millen go after a season or two, Ford kept him on for eight years.

In large part because the Lions have won just one playoff game during his tenure as owner, Ford is not well liked by fans. Actually that's being nice. Quite often the Lions are the subject of Detroit sports talk radio, and many of them think the Lions would win more games with another owner. It's the years of frustration talking.

In 2011, *Forbes* named Ford the NFL's worst owner because the Lions were the only team to lose money in 2010. According to Forbes, an average NFL franchise had generated an 8 percent growth in team value over the past five years, while the Lions had a 3 percent drop.

The Lions went 0–16 in 2008 and 2–14 in 2009. It would be nearly impossible to make money with those records. But the Lions 2010 team was one of the most improved in the NFL, finishing with a 6–10 record and winning four straight to end the season.

William Clay Ford Sr. (center) and team general manager Martin Mayhew (right) talk with head coach Jim Schwartz during an NFL football minicamp on Wednesday, June 24, 2009, in Allen Park, Michigan. (AP Photo/Paul Sancya)

Because he brought the Lions back to Detroit, Ford was named the Michiganian of the Year by the *Detroit News* in 2003. He was inducted into the Michigan Sports Hall of Fame in 2005.

Ford Sr. is the only surviving grandson of auto pioneer Henry Ford. His son, William Clay Ford Jr. who is the executive chairman of Ford Motor Company, serves as the vice chairman of the Lions. Bill Ford Jr. was actively involved in the move of the Lions from the Silverdome in Pontiac back to Detroit, along with the construction of the $500 million Ford Field and the $36 million Lions practice facility in Allen Park, near the Ford Motor headquarters.

The son has more of a presence around the Lions. He's on the sideline prior to games, and it's not uncommon to see him on the sideline at practice. He leaves the Mustang golf cart to his dad. While Ford Sr., is quite a golfer with several holes-in-one to his credit, his son is an avid fly fisherman, enjoys playing hockey and tennis, and is a black belt in Tae Kwon Do.

Football is not just their interest and passion—it's their business, too.

9 A Detroit Tradition

Through the good years and all the bad ones, one tradition remains in Detroit. Since 1934 the Lions have always hosted a game on Thanksgiving Day. It's a tradition like no other.

It all started in 1934, the first year of the Lions' existence. The game was the brainchild of Lions owner G.A. Richards, who had bought the team in 1934 and moved it from Portsmouth, Ohio. He was trying to spark interest in a team that played second banana to the Detroit Tigers.

The Lions played the undefeated world champion Chicago Bears of George Halas in that first Thanksgiving game. The game determined the Western Conference champion. Richards convinced the NBC Radio Network to carry the game, and it was broadcast coast-to-coast on 94 stations.

Prior to that first Thanksgiving game, although the Lions had lost just one game that season, their top gate was 15,000. Against the Bears on Thanksgiving, they drew 26,000 fans to the University of Detroit Stadium and had to turn away thousands.

Despite a pair of Ace Gutowsky touchdowns that day, the Lions lost 19–16 to the Bears. However, a tradition was born.

Thanksgiving Records

The Lions are 33–36–2 in their traditional games on Thanksgiving day. Here are a few of the record highlights:

- Most rushing yardage: 198, Bob Hoernschemeyer, November 23, 1950.
- Most rushing touchdowns: 3, Barry Sanders, November 27, 1997.
- Most passing yards: 410, Scott Mitchell, November 23, 1995.
- Most passing attempts: 46, Shaun Hill, November 25, 2010.
- Most touchdown passes: 4 by Bobby Layne (November 28, 1951), Eric Hipple (November 29, 1985), and Scott Mitchell (November 23, 1995).
- Most touchdown passes by an opponent: 6 by Peyton Manning on November 25, 2004.
- Most return touchdowns: 2 by Jack Christiansen in 1951 and 1954.
- Most field goals: 5 by Jason Hanson on November 27, 2003.

In Detroit the turkey dinner can wait. Many fans start the day attending the annual Thanksgiving Day parade on Woodward Avenue just blocks from Ford Field. A hot dog or two can keep the hunger pangs away during the game, which is always a big deal in Detroit even during less-than-stellar seasons.

The Packers have been a big part of that tradition with 20 visits to Detroit on Thanksgiving. For 13 straight seasons (1951–63), the Lions hosted Green Bay on Turkey Day. Detroit held a 9–3–1 record in that span. Legend has it that Packers coach Vince Lombardi got tired of losing on the holiday and broke the string after 1963.

Unfortunately for the Lions, winning isn't always part of that holiday tradition.

Between 2004 and 2011, the Lions were winless on Turkey Day. In that span they lost to the Indianapolis Colts, Atlanta Falcons, Miami Dolphins, Green Bay (three times), the Tennessee Titans, and New England Patriots.

The 27–10 loss to Miami in 2006 was particularly upsetting because the Dolphins were led by quarterback Joey Harrington who had never lived up to expectations in Detroit.

Crowds flock to the nationally televised affair. The Lions' fans are always optimistic, and quite often tickets to the Thanksgiving game must be purchased early in the season before it sells out.

Over the years more than 3.9 million fans have witnessed the Thanksgiving Day games. They saw the lowest scoring game—a 12–0 loss to Philadelphia in the Mud Bowl in 1968. They saw the most lopsided game—a 45–3 Lions win over Pittsburgh in 1983. They also witnessed seven shutouts, but only one by the Lions (20–0 over the Bears in 1979.)

Back in 1950 they saw Bob Hoernschemeyer set a Thanksgiving rushing record of 198 yards that still stands. He set up a 49–14 win over the New York Yanks. In 1995 they saw Scott Mitchell pass for 410 yards in a 44–38 win over the Vikings.

Through some of the bad times, other NFL owners have threatened to take the game away from Detroit. In the old days, no one wanted the game, but once it became a nationally televised affair, other teams wanted in. You could say they wanted their piece of the pumpkin pie.

The Fords, owners of the Lions, have stood firm. And so the Thanksgiving tradition continues.

10 1935 Championship, A First

Even back in 1935, Lions fans were devoted. On December 15, 12,000 fans braved the sleet and rain at University of Detroit Stadium to watch the Lions win their first championship game 26–7 over the New York Giants, otherwise known as the "Gotham Behemoths."

Professional football was different back then. After the win, fans stormed into the dressing room according to newspaper accounts—there was back-slapping, handshakes, and plenty of cheek kissing (really).

Finally, quarterback Dutch Clark, who was exhausted and not in the mood, asked someone to guard the door. Then owner Dick Richards arrived with a gang of friends. "They stormed in like so many wolves on the prowl," according to a newspaper report. Richards shook hands with every player.

It was quite a game and quite a season. The Lions started the season with a 35–0 win over the Philadelphia Eagles followed by a 10–10 tie with the Chicago Cardinals. They fell to the Dodgers 12–10 in Brooklyn, New York, then beat Boston 17–7. They lost to Green Bay 31–7 in the worst defeat of a George "Potsy" Clark–coached team in four years. But there was still a faint spark of hope that they could make the playoffs. One more defeat and they were done.

The Lions beat the Green Bay Packers 20–10 and tied the Bears 20–20 in Chicago. On Thanksgiving Dutch Clark scored all the Lions' points in a 14–2 win over the Bears. Then they beat the Brooklyn Dodgers 28–0. They clinched a trip to the national championship game when the Bears beat the Cardinals.

Prior to the game, Coach Clark noted that only five of the Lions were guaranteed to start. It's the end of the season, the team is in the title game, and Clark still has guys competing for starting roles. Amazing.

These were the days of leather helmets and no mouth guards. Tackle Jim Steen was one player, but not the only one who left most of his teeth in the dressing room when he took the field.

On that cold and miserable day the Lions scored two touchdowns in the first half thanks to Ace Gutowsky and Dutch Clark. Detroit led 13–0 at the half. But the Giants made it interesting to get within six.

Always Remembered

Several members of the Lions served in World War II. Three of them lost their lives:

- Lt. Charles Behan was killed by Japanese machine gun fire on Okinawa on May 18, 1945.
- Sgt. Alex Ketzko was killed in France with Patch's Seventh Army on December 23, 1944.
- Lt. Chet Wetterlund was killed while flying a navy Hellcat on a night patrol along the New Jersey coast on September 5, 1944.

Midway through the fourth quarter Detroit's George Christensen picked up a partially blocked punt on the Giants' 26 and returned it to the 3-yard line. Then Ernie Caddel, who played the second half with a broken finger, swept in around the right end for the Lions' third touchdown. Detroit's Buddy Parker intercepted a pass on the Giants' 32-yard line and advanced it 22 yards. Three plays later, Parker got in from 3 yards out for a touchdown.

After the 1934 season Richards had promised that if the Lions won the championship in 1935 he would take them to Hawaii. He lived up to his promise, but it wasn't all sand and sun. The Lions, the world champs, played in five exhibition games during the 12,000-mile jaunt that included stops in Denver and Salt Lake City. The Lions scored 182 points in five games, all exhibition wins. They beat the NL All-Stars 33–0, Pacific Coast champions 67–14, League All-Stars 42–7, Green Bay 10–3, and Pop Warner's All-Stars 30–6.

To celebrate the championship win with unique remembrances, the leather covering from the football used in the win was cut into 26 pieces and each piece was mounted on a scroll that was appropriately engraved and given to each player and Coach Clark.

11 Old, Bald, and Still Kicking

In 2009 there was a huge roster turnover following the 0–16 season, and new Lions were everywhere in the locker room. No name tags, but a lot of puzzled "Who's he?" looks. That's when one of newest Lions approached Jason Hanson, thinking he was a coach. After all, he was balding and looked old enough to be the father or, at the very least, the older brother of several of his teammates. Oops.

Hanson completed his 20th season with the Lions in 2011. He was 41, but he still wasn't done with the NFL. His only hope was that the NFL wasn't done with him. He still had two years remaining on his contract.

"Old, bald, and still kicking" was the headline on the *New York Times* profile of Hanson in November 2011. As the Lions all-time leading scorer, Hanson is a lock for the Hall of Fame. It's not just his longevity, it's his production.

After training camp injuries in 2009 and 2010, Hanson had to earn his job in camp prior to the 2011 season. He competed with Dave Rayner, who had finished the 2010 season for Detroit when Hanson was out with a knee injury.

It's not just the cool-under-pressure demeanor of Hanson that kept him around; his accuracy and leg strength have not wavered as he has aged. In 2011 he kicked through a stellar season, nailing 5-of-7 field-goal attempts of 50 yards or longer. Overall he was 24-of-29 on field-goal attempts, and he scored 126 points. For the first time in his career, he kicked field goals of 50 yards or more in three straight games.

Hanson set all kind of marks in the 2011 season. He became the first in the NFL to play 300 career games and register 2,000 points with one team. He was just the eighth player in NFL history to play 300 games.

The 2011 season was special for Hanson because it got him back to the playoffs. After he was drafted by Detroit in the 1992 draft (second round), he and the Lions went to the playoffs in five of his first eight seasons. All was good. Hanson was rubbing shoulders with Barry Sanders, Herman Moore, Brett Perriman, and yes,

Kicker Jason Hanson (4) kicks an extra point out of the hold of Ryan Donahue against the Kansas City Chiefs in the first quarter of a game in Detroit on Sunday, September 18, 2011. (AP Photo/Paul Sancya)

20 Years of Records

In his first 20 seasons with the Lions, kicker Jason Hanson scored 2,016 points with 627 of those coming on extra points.

Hanson has been a machine. In 2011, his 20th season, he kicked 54 extra points, a personal best. In 1993, his second season, he kicked 34 field goals, which remains his career high.

Here are his three best seasons:

1. 1995—132 points, 48 extra points, 28 field goals
2. 1993—130 points, 28 extra points, 34 field goals
3. 2011—126 points, 54 extra points, 24 field goals

Scott Mitchell—all record-setting guys. Wayne Fontes was his first of eight head coaches.

"That was NFL football, it was exciting, you were playing in December, the games mattered, there was intensity to the final weeks instead of climbing in a lifeboat and holding on while the ship goes down," Hanson said.

The lifeboat years stretched from the 2000 season until the big turn-around in 2011. That included the dreadful 0–16 season in 2008.

"Truly, that's what it's like when you're losing. It's kind of good to remember that this is what it's supposed to be like in December. You've got some nerves, you come in during the week, and this is for real. It makes it a lot more meaningful and [you get] ready to work," Hanson said before the Lions clinched their 2011 playoff spot.

Not only did Hanson have to win back his roster spot, he had to adjust to a new holder when rookie punter Ryan Donahue replaced veteran Nick Harris. Whatever it takes to keep kicking.

Let's say Hanson is on the quiet side, but he is also one of the funniest guys in the locker room—a specialist at self-deprecating humor. He's hilarious, but you just wouldn't know it.

He's also a serious athlete who likely holds another franchise record with the best secrets about the Lions for 20 seasons.

12 They Call Him "The Franchise"

At age 23, Matthew Stafford accomplished something only three other quarterbacks in the history of the NFL have done. He threw for 5,000 yards in his third Lions season—which also happened to be his first complete 16-game season due to injuries his first two years. It seems he's just getting started.

Stafford grew up in Dallas admiring Troy Aikman, John Elway, and Brett Favre. The Lions quarterback knows what it takes to make the leap from good to great in the ranks of NFL quarterbacks. It's all about winning in the playoffs.

"They do whatever it takes to win. That's what you have to do, whether it's go out there and run, throw, whatever you have to do, get your team in position to win, that's what I'm going to do," Stafford said with just the right measure of cockiness and confidence.

Stafford got his first shot at the playoffs on January 7, 2012, facing Drew Brees, who had also thrown for 5,000 yards in 2011, and the New Orleans Saints. It didn't work out as planned for the Lions' gunslinger, but he expects to have many more postseason opportunities. After all, he was young. He left Georgia at age 21 for the 2009 draft where he was Detroit's first overall pick.

To end the 2011 season, Stafford threw for 520 yards in a loss at Green Bay, hitting 5,038 yards. "I don't think you can put a number on anything. I definitely expected him to bounce back from his injuries his first two years and his first full year starting, and that's exactly what he did," Lions center Dominic Raiola said. "I said it all along, the sky's the limit for this kid."

Stafford admitted 5,000 is a "lofty" number. Then he attributed the milestone to his teammates.

"We were just trying to do whatever it took to win. We had to throw the ball probably more than we wanted to this year, it resulted in wins—enough to get us into the playoffs and that's what it's all about," Stafford said. "Obviously, that's a team accomplishment. It doesn't just happen for me you've got to have guys out there getting open making plays after they catch it, guys up front blocking, it was a total team effort. It's great to be a part of it," he added.

Stafford and the Lions offense discovered in the 2011 season that they have the tools to get out of most any situation.

"It hasn't just been numbers with Matt, it's been comebacks in games, it's been adversity, and it's the manner in which he's done it. Even considering where we've been—you know, losing Jahvid [Best] and [Mikel] Leshoure early in training camp and early in the season put a little bit more pressure on him to do it.... Those numbers can get skewed for a lot of reasons," Coach Jim Schwartz said. "I don't think that's the case with Matthew."

Stafford was been calm under pressure all season, leading four comebacks from deficits of 13 or more points. Two-minute drill? Bring it on.

Ah, the Cleveland Game

Matthew Stafford's rookie season was mostly forgettable as the Lions finished with a 2–14 record. The young quarterback missed half a dozen games with a shoulder injury. However, one game that will never be forgotten is the 38–37 win over Cleveland. The Lions were down 37–31 with zero seconds remaining due to a Browns' penalty. Stafford was down on the sideline with medical personnel attending to his non-throwing shoulder, which had been dislocated. It looked like he was done, but he got up, brushed past the doctors and trainers, and went back in the game, throwing a touchdown to tie the game with Jason Hanson icing the win with the extra point.

Stafford was mic'd for the game, and it proved to be great theater. He also proved just how tough he can be.

Matthew Stafford (9) throws a pass during a Week 10 game against the Chicago Bears on November 13, 2011, in Chicago. (AP Photo/David Stluka)

Stafford seems to have an answer for everything.

"That's what we try to do. We have great talent around me, which is the No. 1 thing you have to have. Guys who understand zone and do something with it after they catch it, we've got it all," Stafford said. "Hopefully we can go out there, execute at a high level, and see what happens."

Stafford's success, of course, depends on others around him. That may be the biggest change from his rookie season to his third season. "I'd say the most important thing for his progression is players around him—having Calvin and Nate and Titus [Young] and [Maurice] Stovall and Rashied [Davis] and [Brandon] Pettigrew and [Tony] Scheffler and Jahvid [Best]," Schwartz said. "It's a lot different than when he was out there as a rookie without as much support. If you really talk about his progression, you have to look at the progression of the offense along with him, particularly at the talent level."

But it's not just the changes on the offensive roster that helped Stafford. In his rookie season, the defensive line was a mish-mash and perhaps the biggest question mark on the team other than the defensive backfield.

"Part of Matt's progression as a player is our building of the defense and having the patience that you can throw a ball away and knowing that we're not going to give up a touchdown on the next drive and the game would be over," Schwartz said. "That's part of it also."

Continuity is another factor. Stafford had been in the same offense under the same coordinator since he first stepped foot in the Lions' practice facility. "I think that has something to do with it…. We have a lot of returning players and guys that understand the offense. When you've got guys that understand the offense, when you get guys who know what to do, they can play fast and relaxed and really let their ability come out," Stafford said.

With a leader like Stafford, who works as hard or harder than all of them, it helps. "We all know the talent, we know the other things that come with it—the smarts, another year under his belt, he's hungry, he's' extra hungry," Raiola said just prior to the 2011 season. "I think he's working extremely hard, not that he didn't do it before, but he's hungry and it's showing."

When it was over, Stafford had his 5,038 yards and his first trip to the playoffs. Some of his teammates call him "The Franchise." And with good reason.

13 The Smell of Success

It wasn't unusual to arrive at the Silverdome office in the 1990s and find Charlie Sanders outside at a barbecue grill. It always smelled heavenly. Sanders, the Hall of Fame Lions tight end, has a thing with barbecue. At Ford Field he has his own Charlie Sanders Hall of Fame Barbecue where pulled barbecue pork or chicken are the specialties that feed hungry fans.

It's all yummy and good, but cooking is not what got Charlie Sanders into the Pro Football Hall of Fame. He was voted in on February 3, 2007, and was only the seventh tight end inducted.

Sanders, who was from North Carolina, was selected by Detroit in the third round of the 1968 draft. And Detroit has been home ever since. His playing career as a tight end stretched from 1968–77, and along the way he had 336 career receptions and was known as a superior blocker as well as receiver. Sanders was chosen for the Pro Bowl as a rookie and seven times total (1968–71 and 1974–76). He was named to the NFL 1970s All-Decade Team and is a member of the North Carolina Sports Hall of Fame. In 2008, he was also chosen as a member of the Lions 75th Anniversary All-Time Team. And he was inducted into the Michigan Sports Hall of Fame in 1990.

Sanders maintained close ties with the Lions through the years. After retirement, he spent seven years with the team as a radio color commentator (1983–88, 1997), eight years as an assistant coach working with tight ends and receivers (1989–96) and started in 1998 as a player personnel scout and assistant director of pro personnel. A regular around the practice facility, Sanders maintains his trim figure and looks like he could still take the field—just like the playing days, when he missed just a dozen games in his 10-year career.

In his Hall of Fame acceptance speech, Sanders shed some light on his upbringing in rural North Carolina. He said he challenged himself early on, even if it was work or chores as the opponent.

He said it best that day at Canton, Ohio: "The country, as I refer to it, is a place where a kid could be judged, his character could be judged, by how fast he was able to work alongside the adults. It was a place where your family pet may have been the runt from the pig litter. It was a place where your pet could have been a chick kicked to the side by mother hen.

"Life in the country was simple. I learned a lot there. The main thing I learned, you've heard it—it takes a village to raise a child. Well, in that village, there were a lot of adults. There were a lot of aunts, uncles, and cousins. And it was everybody's responsibility for your upbringing. Sometimes you were disciplined by people you didn't know. And the worst spankings you got were not from your parents. It was all for one, one for all."

His upbringing explains who he is.

"I am not that self-proclaimed Hall of Famer who desired to be in sports. I am a guy that liked a challenge, and I challenged myself with the understanding that winning is finishing," he said in the speech.

Sanders, the father of nine with his wife, Georgianna, ended his speech at Canton with a story that brought a tear to the eye.

"You see, my brothers and I lost my mother when I was only two. Of all the things I've done in football, and there have been a lot, there's one thing that I really, really regretted. Many times I've seen athletes, college, professional, often look into a television and say, 'Hi, Mom.' I always thought that was special and always something I'd want to do but couldn't.

"So I take this time right here, right now in Canton, Ohio, at the Pro Football Hall of Fame to say, 'Hi, Mom. Thank you for the ultimate sacrifice. This day belongs to you, for it was written.' I want to thank you all enjoying the best day of my life and may God bless you."

There you go. That's Charlie Sanders, a Hall of Famer and much more.

14 The Blond Bomber

Quarterback Bobby Layne may be known more for his curse than for the three championships he helped bring to the Lions. Even then, the curse could be legend or fact.

It goes like this. In 1958, the Lions were coming off their third NFL championship in six years with Layne at quarterback. They lost the first game of 1958, then tied the second 13–13.

That was that. Layne was traded to the Pittsburgh Steelers and replaced with Tobin Rote.

Legend has it that on Layne's way out of Detroit, he said the Lions won't win for the next 50 years. The Lions went 4–7–1 in 1958 and in the 50 years since have had just one playoff victory. In 2008, the 50th year of the curse, the Lions set the NFL record with a 0–16 season.

Hall of Fame quarterback Bobby Layne. (Courtesy Pro Football Hall of Fame via AP Images)

The hard-living, swashbuckling, blond-headed Layne died in 1986 shortly before his 60th birthday, and his secret of whether or not he cursed the Lions was buried with him.

Joe Schmidt, one of Layne's teammates, doesn't know if Layne said it, but he wouldn't have been surprised if he did. Schmidt never understood why Layne was traded. The Lions haven't won a championship since.

Layne arrived in Detroit in 1950 in a trade. He was reunited with Doak Walker, his teammate in their days at Highland Park High School in Texas. (Coincidentally, it is the same school attended by Lions quarterback Matthew Stafford.)

Layne led the Lions to a championship in 1952, their first in 17 years. He followed it up with another in 1953. A three-peat? No, but close. The Lions lost to the Cleveland Browns in the 1954 NFL Championship Game.

Late in the 1957 season, Layne broke his leg in three places during an on-field pileup. Tobin Rote finished the season and led the Lions to the championship.

Layne was voted into the Pro Football Hall of Fame in 1967 and the Texas Longhorn Hall of Honor in 1963. In 1999 he was ranked No. 52 on *The Sporting News'* list of football's 100 greatest players. In 1995, *Sports Illustrated* called him "the toughest quarterback who ever lived."

Layne's statistics were not gaudy. His bravery and leadership that set him apart from the rest. Many of his passes were of the wounded-duck variety. With the game on the line he was golden. He's been credited with creating the two-minute offense.

He was one of the last in the NFL to play without a facemask. He was that tough.

Layne played for the Chicago Bears (1948), New York Bulldogs (1949), Detroit Lions (1950–58), and the Pittsburgh Steelers (1958–62). After retiring from 15 seasons in the NFL, Layne held the career records for both passes attempted (3,700) and completed (1,814), as well as yards gained passing (26,768) and passing touchdowns (196).

In the Lions' 1952 championship win, Layne threw four interceptions. When the Lions won the title in 1953, he was picked off twice. He still holds the Lions' postseason record for most interceptions in a game with six in the 1954 Championship Game that the Lions lost.

He also still holds many of the career passing records for the Lions including yards (15,710), touchdowns (118), attempts (2,193), completions (1,074), interceptions (118), and most interceptions in a season (23).

Layne was also known for his off-the-field heavy drinking which, again, has grown legendary throughout the years. He was often in tandem with teammate Alex Karras.

He is reported to have said that if he had known how long he was going to live, he would have taken better care of himself. His friend and neighbor in Dallas, Mickey Mantle, also used that line.

15 Another NFL Championship

Back in 1952, the Lions were starved for a championship. They won their first championship in 1935, and fans were getting a little antsy for another. After decades of modern-day futility, it's a little difficult to imagine. That's the way it was, according to newspaper accounts, when the 1952 Lions (10–3) headed to Cleveland Stadium for the NFL Championship Game on December 28, 1952.

Cleveland had won five straight titles before losing the Championship Game the previous year, so the Lions knew it would be tough. Additionally, nine of the 33 players on the Detroit roster were rookies. The Lions, who had smashed all attendance records that season, were favored. The championship game drew 50,934 fans in Cleveland that day.

It had been a tough season for the Lions with the turning point occurring in the third game at Briggs Stadium (later known as Tiger Stadium) when the Lions were embarrassed 28–0 by San Francisco.

How bad was it that day? Reports are that it was worse than the score indicated.

Under Coach Buddy Parker, the Lions regrouped and won eight of their last nine to force themselves into a playoff for the divisional title with the Los Angeles Rams. Mission accomplished. Then it was on to the title game, not yet known as the Super Bowl.

It was a dramatic 17–7 win for Detroit whose offense was run by future Hall of Famer Bobby Layne. The Lions scored on a 67-yard run by Doak Walker who took a handoff from Layne, ran through a right tackle hole created by Gus Cifelli, zigzagged through the secondary, and used Cloyce Box as a screen downfield to dodge the last two Browns and give the Lions a 14–0 third-quarter lead.

On that day, Layne overshadowed "Automatic" Otto Graham, the Browns' quarterback. The Lions' first touchdown came courtesy of a two-yard sneak by Layne.

It was a running game with the Lions rolling up 258 total yards, and just 59 of those were passing. The Lions didn't fumble the ball, and Layne did not throw an interception.

While Layne got much of the credit, the Lions defense played a special game that day. They allowed the Browns inside the Lions' 20-yard line only four times. And so the Lions celebrated after their 17-year championship drought.

It was a big deal for the Lions, many of whom had off-season jobs, because as the winners they each pocketed $2,274.77. The Browns got the losing share of $1,712.49 each.

Coach Buddy Parker had played on the 1935 championship team, so the win was just a little sweeter.

Within 30 minutes of the final play, Layne was in his car and headed back to his home in Texas. When asked how far he would drive that day, he said he would drive until he got tired. Apparently a championship provided a little adrenaline even back in the old days.

16 Scott Mitchell's Ups and Downs

As a beginner pilot, Scott Mitchell routinely flew in and out of Oakland Pontiac Airport about 10 miles west of the Silverdome.

Luckily, Mitchell was a good learner because one day as he was approaching the airport, one of the busiest in Michigan, all the radio controls in his small plane went dead. All contact with the tower was gone, and Mitchell was thousands of feet in the air.

In that case, he had been instructed to go to a certain altitude and circle, waiting for the runways to clear. So he did, and they did, and all was well. He survived a life-and-death audible of sorts.

Mitchell, an affable quarterback, loved to share his flying stories. Up in the air, the pressure was different. Back on earth, there's no pressure quite like that of being a Detroit Lions quarterback.

Mitchell knew that well. He was a Lions' quarterback for five long seasons (1994–98). He was skewered on Detroit sports talk radio 365 days a year, especially in 1996 and 1997.

He had the arm and the size (6'6", 240 pounds) but was inconsistent. By far his best season came in 1995. The records he set in that season stood until young Matthew Stafford smashed them in 2011. Mitchell did hold Lions franchise records for passing yards in a season (4,338), passing touchdowns in a season (32), passer rating in a season (92.3), and 300-yard passing games in a season (five).

By far 1995 was his standout season with Mitchell passing for 32 touchdowns and just 12 interceptions. Those 32 touchdowns topped the mark of 26 set by the Lions' great Bobby Layne in 1951.

Mitchell had a little help with running back Barry Sanders opening up the passing game. His receivers included Herman Moore, Brett Perriman, and Johnnie Morton. In fact, in 1995

Moore (1,686) and Perriman (1,488) combined for more than 3,000 receiving yards.

Following that 10–6 season, the Lions got thumped in the first round of the playoffs at Philadelphia 58–37.

Mitchell and the Lions could never bring back that magic from 1995. In 1996 they went 5–11 and finished 1997 with a 9–7 record. Mitchell did lead them to the playoffs in 1997 when they lost 20–10 at Tampa Bay and Mitchell was carried off the field on a stretcher. It wasn't serious.

In training camp while preparing for the 1998 campaign, Mitchell was on fire. At the end of camp, Coach Bobby Ross said Mitchell had thrown just five bad balls in all of camp—a pretty remarkable number for any quarterback.

But Mitchell couldn't carry that into the regular season and was benched after two games—a loss at Green Bay and an overtime loss to Cincinnati at the Silverdome in which he threw two interceptions and zero touchdowns. Charlie Batch got the nod from Ross. Mitchell had lost his chance.

Mitchell was a character who would occasionally fake-limp through the locker room trying to throw off the writers. Other than the 1995 season, one of his claims to fame was the Halloween party

Touchdown Tommy Scores Three

Touchdown Tommy Vardell lived up to his nickname in a 38–15 win over Minnesota on November 16, 1997, when he scored three touchdowns. All three came on 1-yard handoffs from quarterback Scott Mitchell.

That matched half his touchdown output for the season. Vardell had a dozen touchdowns in two seasons with Detroit. He got his nickname after scoring four TDs for Stanford against Notre Dame—all on 1-yard bursts.

Before and since, only one Lion has run for more touchdowns in a single game. Barry Sanders once scored four touchdowns in a game. Sanders also ran in for three touchdowns in a game five times.

in 1996. It was no coincidence that it happened a few days after Mitchell had been benched by Fontes during a 35–7 home loss to the New York Giants. Mitchell had gone 9-of-19 for 71 yards and three interceptions.

Mitchell dressed as Coach Wayne Fontes, smoking a big cigar, wearing Mickey Mouse ears (Fontes had been photographed wearing the Mickey Mouse hat for a charitable promotion), padding for a big belly, and a Lions sweatshirt to top it off.

Mitchell as Fontes called himself "a big buck" because he was the biggest target. At least we knew he had a sense of humor.

After 1998, Mitchell finished his career with the Baltimore Ravens and Cincinnati Bengals. In 2008, he took over as the head football coach at his alma mater, Springville High School in Utah.

17 Time for a Turn-Around

After 10 consecutive losing seasons, the Lions felt they were on the brink, finishing 2010 with four straight wins, including two on the road.

For 2011, they had the pieces in place. They felt they could compete with any team in the NFL. The offense was led by quarterback Matthew Stafford, looking to play his first full season, and Calvin Johnson, who just needed a chance to prove he was the NFL's best wide receiver. On defense, the strength was the line.

The Lions had been talking about climbing over that invisible hump since they finished 2008 with that god-awful 0–16 record. That was some wake-up call. It created a shake-up in which Martin Mayhew was promoted to general manager. He, in turn, hired Jim

Schwartz, who had no head coaching experience, to make the turn-around in Detroit.

The roster needed to be almost totally revamped.

A new attitude was essential. A new look, too. They painted the walls in the locker room; changed up locker assignments, blending in offense and defense; and created a parking policy that gave the best spots to the veterans. It's all in the details.

Throw in a little luck and it was time to get started. The new leaders got off to a slow start in 2009 with a 2–14 season. It wasn't exactly what they were hoping for, but they stuck to their plan. This leadership team wasn't looking for a short-term fix, they were looking to build a championship team for the long haul.

After 2010, there was a sense the team was definitely headed in the right direction with a good core group of youngsters mixed in with a wily group of veterans.

The 2011 season didn't end until the Lions lost 45–28 at New Orleans in a wild-card playoff game. That was one sign this bunch was moving in the right direction. They hadn't been to a playoff game since the 1999 season, but they finished the regular season 10–6, good enough for a wild-card berth.

They started red-hot, winning their first five, then they limped to a 7–5 record and finished 3–1, for the 10–6 season record.

Offensively, the Lions shattered franchise passing and receiving records thanks to the efforts of Stafford and Calvin Johnson. Defensively, they struggled in the final two games—a loss at Green Bay to end the regular season and the playoff loss. The secondary had opened the season fine, but they closed it with fans shaking their heads in dismay.

It wasn't the Lions' goal to just get to the playoffs; they wanted to win in the postseason, too. Like they say, one out of two ain't bad.

"I think it was an important year for us. I certainly wouldn't call it, I certainly wouldn't classify it as a good year," Coach Jim

Working Out on their Own

During the NFL lockout in the off-season prior to the 2011 season, the Lions players organized their own workouts at Birmingham Detroit Country Day's $6 million indoor facility. They averaged about 30 players per session with two weeks of four sessions each week. Kyle Vanden Bosch, Dominic Raiola, and Matthew Stafford were the ringleaders.

It was the only chance that the rookies had to meet their new teammates before the start of training camp. Running back Mikel Leshoure and wide receiver Titus Young took advantage of the opportunity. One day Barry Sanders, yes that Barry Sanders, was seen walking the corridors of the school during the workouts. It had nothing to do with the team, though. He was there to see one of his children.

Schwartz said. "Our expectations are high, but it was an important year for us. It was something—getting to the playoffs—that hadn't been done for a long time, and it was an important step, not for the organization and the city but for individual players to have gone through that."

The turn-around from the start of the 2008 season to 2011 was huge. For the 2008 opener only seven starters made it through to 2011—wide receiver Calvin Johnson, running back Kevin Smith, left tackle Jeff Backus, center Dominic Raiola, right guard Stephen Peterman, kicker Jason Hanson, and long snapper Don Muhlbach. Cliff Avril, Andre Fluellen, and Gosder Cherilus were on the 2008 roster but buried on the depth chart.

"We're on the rise. I don't know what else to say right now. It was a fun year, and I look forward to big things from this group, this team," Raiola said when it was over. "We have a good locker room. The front office, the coaching staff really tightened this locker room up. We've got a good locker room. I look forward to big things."

18 One Playoff Win in 54 Years

During the years when the Lions couldn't win after getting into the playoffs and the stretch when they simply couldn't make it to the postseason, this was a win that stood out.

At the time, who would have thought it would be so long before the Lions could win another playoff game? It happened on January 5, 1992, after the Lions had won the NFC Central with a 12–4 record. It wasn't just a win, it was a 38–6 shellacking of the Dallas Cowboys at the Pontiac Silverdome.

It was the seventh straight win for the Lions after their offensive lineman, Mike Utley, had been paralyzed in a freak play in a win over the Los Angeles Rams on November 17. Utley had left the field on a stretcher, giving his teammates the thumbs-up sign.

The remainder of the season was dedicated to Utley, who, at the time of the playoffs, was at a rehabilitation hospital in Denver. Before the game, some of his teammates called him. He offered inspiration.

In that game, the Cowboys' defense was stacked to stop Barry Sanders. So quarterback Erik Kramer took advantage and completed 29-of-38 passes for 341 yards, three touchdowns, and no interceptions. Sanders carried a dozen times for 69 yards, including a 47-yard touchdown run in the fourth quarter.

The Lions' defense held Dallas to 276 total yards and forced two fumbles and had two interceptions. Steve Beuerlein was 7-of-13 for 91 yards and one interception before Troy Aikman (11-of-16, 114 yards, one interception) stepped in. The Cowboys were held to a pair of 28-yard field goals by Ken Willis.

The Lions scored first when Kramer connected with Willie Green for a 31-yard touchdown pass play in the first quarter. The

Cowboys kicked the first of two field goals to narrow the gap. Then Mel Jenkins intercepted Beuerlein and returned the ball 41 yards for a touchdown. Eddie Murray kicked a 36-yard field goal for Detroit before Green caught a 9-yard touchdown pass (his second of the game) and rookie Herman Moore caught a 7-yard touchdown pass. Sanders finished up the scoring on a 47-yard scamper.

The win boosted the Lions franchise playoff record to 7–4. It was the furthest the Lions had advanced in the playoffs since 1957 when they won their fourth NFL championship. It was their first playoff game since 1983 when they had lost a heart-breaker 24–23 at San Francisco. They had won the NFC Central that season with a 9–7 record.

After the 38–6 win, a headline in *The Oakland Press* read, "Just coincidence? Or are the Lions destiny's darlings?"

It was the first time that head coach Wayne Fontes, who was hired in 1988, had brought the Lions to the playoffs. Herman Moore was a rookie wide receiver. It was to be his only playoff win—the same for Sanders who was in his first playoff game. It was the final game ever for starting left guard Eric Andolsek who was killed in a freak accident while working in his yard the following June.

It's a game that has withstood the test of time. What had the Lions ever done in the playoffs? Well, they had this one win to look back on. Because the next week they lost 41–10 to the Washington Redskins.

That one playoff win was special, but the glow didn't last.

19 At Last Back to the Playoffs

It had been so long. Capping off a 10–6 turn-around season, the Lions made it to the playoffs in 2011 for the first time since the 1999 season. That's a long time for any NFL team.

Here was a team that three years previously had set an NFL record for being the only team that lost every game in a season. Their 0–16 record brought in major changes—a new general manager, a new coach, and a mostly new roster.

It was an accomplishment to get so far in just three seasons. The goal wasn't just to get to the playoffs, it was to win and win again. They came up short, losing 45–28 in New Orleans against the Saints who had a perfect record at the Superdome that season.

Quarterback Matthew Stafford and Pro Bowl wide receiver Calvin Johnson made their playoff debuts. They may have had butterflies, but it did not show. The two put on an aerial display for the second straight game. The previous week, the Lions had ended the regular season with a loss in Green Bay despite the 520 passing yards by Stafford and 244 yards and one touchdown caught by Johnson. In New Orleans, the dynamic duo remained red-hot with Stafford completing 28-of-43 attempts for 380 yards, two passing touchdowns, and one where he dove around a pylon. Johnson finished his first playoff game with a wild-card playoff record 12 catches for 211 yards.

The Lions won three of their last four games with the Christmas Eve win over San Diego at Ford Field clinching a playoff spot. In the final game, a win at Lambeau Field against the Packers would have given them a five seed. Since they lost (they hadn't beat the Packers on the road since 1991), they settled for the No. 6 seed.

The week leading up to the wild-card game, the Lions insisted it didn't matter who they played. They knew that to be the best you must beat the best.

A controversial call late in the second quarter could have cost them the game. No one will ever know. Willie Young forced a fumble, and linebacker Justin Durant scooped up the ball and headed toward the promised land but stopped when he heard a whistle. It was an inadvertent whistle from an official who thought Brees had thrown an incomplete pass. A touchdown there would have given the Lions a 21–7 lead and changed the complexion of the game. It was the second week in a row that the officials had cost the Lions a touchdown. In Green Bay, rookie wide receiver Titus Young clearly had both feet down when he caught a Stafford pass in the end zone, but he was called out and the Lions were out of challenges. So the Lions were left to think about what might have been.

The Lions' defense struggled, allowing the Saints to set a playoff record with 626 total yards. Drew Brees was 33-of-43 for 466 yards and three touchdowns. The teams combined for 1,038 yards, tying an NFL playoff record set by Buffalo and Miami on December 30, 1995.

The Lions were still stunned two days later. They went to New Orleans to win the first playoff game for the Lions since 1991—and they came up short.

Their goal is that it shouldn't be a big deal when they get into the playoffs. It should happen every season. "A loss like this makes us want to return to the playoffs even more," defensive end Kyle Vanden Bosch said. "It will be no surprise to everyone when the Detroit Lions start to make the playoffs each and every year."

20 One Loss, Multiple Changes

Of all the Lions' losses through the years, one had more impact than any other. On December 24, 2000, the Lions needed a win over the Chicago Bears at the Silverdome to get into the playoffs. A win would get them in and keep out the St. Louis Rams, the defending Super Bowl champs. Mistakes and turnovers sealed the Lions' fate that day.

Many people call it the Paul Edinger game. The Bears kicker nailed a career-long 54-yard field goal with two seconds remaining to break a tie and beat the Lions who had been 10-point favorites.

Not only was it a tough 23–20 loss it was a game that changed everything for the Lions. Gary Moeller coached that game after taking over nine games into the season for Bobby Ross, who unexpectedly resigned. Moeller had led the Lions to wins in four of the six previous games.

The players loved playing for him despite the fact he was tougher on them and demanded more accountability than Ross, who was nicknamed the General. In fact, maybe that's why they liked playing for Moeller.

"Well, my take on it was we were pretty good, we had played pretty good that game, at the end we made some mistakes and they capitalized. He bombed a 54 to beat us. Everyone was fired and 10 years of oblivion," said Jason Hanson, the only remaining Lion who was on that team.

At quarterback that day was Charlie Batch, who took a helmet hit in the second quarter and was replaced by Stoney Case. Bears quarterback Shane Matthews busted his thumb in the first half and was replaced by Cade McNown.

Afterward, Lions wide receiver Johnnie Morton wondered out loud if the Lions were jinxed. Herman Moore, who was wide open and lost a ball in the lights, had seen it before and told reporters, "It's always something."

The Bears scored their final 10 points off two Detroit turnovers, including a Case pass that R.W. McQuarters intercepted and returned 61 yards for a touchdown. Hanson tied the score with a 26-yard field goal with two minutes left. But the Lions' defense couldn't stop the Bears from getting into field-goal position.

No playoffs for the 2000 Lions, who finished 9–7.

"I remember it was kind of a stunning loss. I think we had them beat.... A lot of things were, 'Wow, what are we doing?' We had played pretty good until then, then a bunch of errors," Hanson said. "That was a culmination of years when they got rid of everyone. We were decent. I think the effort was to stop being just okay and try to be one of the elite teams."

The Lions were getting to the playoffs—in 1993, 1994, 1995, 1997, 1999—but not winning playoff games.

Hanson remembers the 1997 season when Barry Sanders ran for 2,053 yards and the Lions made it to the playoffs. "That was NFL football, it was exciting, you were playing in December, the games mattered, there was intensity to the final weeks instead of climbing in a lifeboat and holding on while the ship goes down," Hanson said.

"Truly, that's what it's like when you're losing. It's kind of good to remember that, this is what it's supposed to be like in December. You've got some nerves, you come in during the week, and this is for real. It makes it a lot more meaningful and [you get] ready to work," he added.

That loss on Christmas Eve 2000 changed everything about those Lions. Turns out it was Moeller's last game. He was fired by Matt Millen who was hired after longtime general manager Chuck Schmidt was fired. The Millen era had begun.

The Lions just wanted to win a playoff game and couldn't even get close to a winning season. They wouldn't have another shot at the playoffs until 11 years later.

21 Forget the Millen Era

Remember when Matt Millen arrived in Detroit in 2001? The Lions' fans welcomed him with open arms. He was the FOX broadcaster who excelled at analyzing NFL games. In his 12-year career as a player with the Oakland Raiders, San Francisco 49ers, and Washington Redskins, he played on four Super Bowl championship teams. He had a Super Bowl ring from each of the three teams for which he played.

Overlooked was the fact he had zero experience as an NFL team executive. No scouting, no player development, nothing. Lions fans loved him, though.

Their beloved Lions had been to the playoffs in 1993, 1994, 1995, 1997, and 1999, but they hadn't won a single playoff game since 1991. Millen would turn that around, right?

The former linebacker talked a good game, which explains why the Fords hired him to run their franchise. He was the cool guy. Remember? He wore a shirt and tie to work but completed his look by wearing sneakers instead of wingtips. He was quirky, and he was Detroit's.

A carpenter in his spare time, before his first draft as the Lions' general manager, Millen routinely wore a cap that said, "Measure twice, cut once." Well, certainly that would be a good credo for a GM, too, wouldn't it?

The Three Worst Millen Draft Picks

Matt Millen ran eight Lions' drafts (2001–08). Even though he had a competent player personnel department, he reportedly often went with his gut feelings. It's difficult to narrow it down, but here are his three worst draft picks.

1. QB Joey Harrington (first round, third overall in 2002). In four seasons he never led the team to a winning record. In his best season (2004), he threw 19 touchdowns and a dozen interceptions. His eternal optimism earned him the nickname "Joey Blue Skies."
2. WR Charles Rogers (first round, second overall in 2003). The Michigan State product had substance abuse issues. He was a bust due to a pair of broken collarbones in 2003 and 2004. During 2005, he was suspended four games for his third violation of the NFL's substance abuse policy. He was cut in 2006.
3. WR Mike Williams (first round, 10th overall, 2005). Jaws dropped at the announcement on draft day. The previous year the Lions had drafted WR Roy Williams in the first round. The team had dire needs, and they weren't at wide receiver. Williams had been out of football for a year and was a huge risk for a first-round pick.

You might not be ready to admit it, but Matt Millen's hiring was roundly applauded. To truly enjoy being a Lions' fan going forward, however, you must forget the Matt Millen era and the eight years he held the Lions hostage.

Forget about him, forget about how he kept his home in Pennsylvania and rode his motorcycle back on weekends. You always thought being an NFL GM was a 24/7 job and, of course, you're right. So forget that Millen looked on it as a 40-hour-per-week gig.

Forget about his 31–97 record, the worst eight-year record in the history of the modern day NFL. Forget that in his first three seasons (2001–03) the Lions failed to win a road game, going 0–24 before winning at Chicago to start the 2004 season. Forget about his horrific drafts.

When the Lions traded 2006 first-round pick Ernie Sims in April 2010, only three of Millen's first-round picks remained—Calvin Johnson, Jeff Backus, and Gosder Cherilus. No players remained on the 2011 Lions roster who had been drafted by Millen from 2002–05. Those players would have been in the prime of their careers.

Forget that Millen was the second-highest paid GM in the NFL. Forget that the *Wall Street Journal* reported that NFL executives admitted in private that Millen "has made more bad draft decisions than anyone else in two centuries." Forget that after four seasons and a 16–48 record he was given a five-year contract extension at the start of the 2005 season. After a 3–13 record in 2006, William Clay Ford Sr. announced Millen would be around at least another year.

Forget the "Fire Millen" chants that popped up during Red Wings games and even at a University of Michigan basketball game. Many of the young Wolverines didn't even know who Millen was.

Forget that he was the architect of the 0–16 season in 2008 even though he wasn't around to see it through. He was fired on September 24, 2008. Forget the coaches he hired—the three M's of Marty Mornhinweg (5–27), Steve Mariucci (15–28), and Rod Marinelli (10–38). Forget that he stripped the Lions' cupboards bare. Forget that it took years to replenish the talent after his eight bad drafts.

Forget the Matt Millen era, it's better that way.

22 Joey Not a Favorite

Joey Harrington was never well liked in Detroit. That puts it mildly. Perhaps it was his 18–37 record as a starting quarterback for the Lions. Perhaps it was his cheerful attitude that earned him the nickname of "Joey Blue Skies."

Whatever the reason, he was not a good fit for the Lions or vice-versa. In his four seasons with the Lions, he had three head coaches and several position coaches. He was booed often. Was it Joey? Or was it the fact that the Lions were always in transition and he was surrounded by talent that was perhaps overrated?

Harrington was not especially well liked by his teammates, either. It's tough for a quarterback to be successful if his teammates don't like him. Cornerback Dre Bly told NFL Network's Rich Eisen that he blamed Harrington for the firing of Steve Mariucci. Bly later apologized to the Lions but not to Harrington. And at one point Harrington told a team official that he hated everybody on the team and they hated him.

Harrington was drafted with the third overall pick in the 2002 draft by Matt Millen, the Lions' general manager. Not everyone in the personnel department agreed with the pick, but Millen made it anyway.

At Oregon as a three-year starter, Harrington threw for 6,289 yards and 53 touchdowns. He finished his college career with a 25–3 record. With the Ducks he had been a confident downfield thrower. Lions' fans rarely saw that confidence.

In his rookie season (2002), he took over for Mike McMahon late in the Week 1 loss against Miami and became the starter shortly after that. He finished the season with a 50.1 completion percentage, 12 touchdowns against 16 interceptions, and a 59.9 quarterback rating. No wonder the Lions were 3–13 that year.

In what turned out to be his final game with the Lions, the last game of the 2005 season, Harrington threw three touchdown passes in a 35–21 loss at the Pittsburgh Steelers. He completed 17-of-33 passes for 212 yards with a 102.1 rating that day. But for that season he had thrown just a dozen touchdowns, which matched up exactly with his dozen interceptions. He had been benched twice that season and replaced by Jeff Garcia.

After the end of the 2005 season, the Harrington situation became a little more odd.

In February 2006, Millen said the team would approach the off-season with Harrington as the starting quarterback. A month later Lions head coach Rod Marinelli, starting his first season in Detroit, said the team was moving on without Harrington even though technically he was still on the roster.

The team signed quarterback free agents Jon Kitna and Josh McCown. It was Marinelli's decision for Harrington not to report for off-season workouts.

It was a bit of a surprise because Marinelli brought in Mike Martz as his offensive coordinator. At first Martz wanted to tear down Harrington and then build him back up. In his career, Martz had developed less talented quarterbacks like Trent Green (who was an eighth-round pick), Kurt Warner (undrafted), and Marc Bulger (sixth-round pick). He never got the chance with Harrington.

The Lions traded Harrington to the Miami Dolphins. After one season in Miami (2006), Harrington was briefly with the Atlanta Falcons and the New Orleans Saints.

He made news in the summer of 2011 when he was struck by an SUV while riding his bike near his home in Portland, Oregon. He suffered a broken collarbone and a punctured lung. He probably didn't get any get-well cards from Detroit.

23 Biggest Draft Bust

Charles Rogers was clearly a bust as the second overall pick in the 2003 draft. As much as Lions' fans decry Matt Millen's drafts, it's quite possible that this was not Millen's fault. At least not totally.

Rogers had the opportunities in the NFL but never lived up to expectations. The Saginaw native had smashed several receiving records at Michigan State, including setting the school record with the most touchdowns in a career with 27. He was the winner of the 2002 Fred Biletnikoff Award which goes annually to the best wide receiver in college football. (Calvin Johnson won it in 2006 at Georgia Tech.) The 6'4" receiver was compared to Randy Moss.

On the field Rogers was all of that. Off the field he tested positive for marijuana twice while at Michigan State. Turns out it was a sign of things to come. At the NFL Combine, he tested for excess water, which is often considered a masking agent.

Surely it was a red flag, but the Lions didn't let it stop them from selecting Rogers, a receiver with the speed to throw fear into the hearts of cornerbacks. They saw Rogers as a good complement to quarterback Joey Harrington, the No. 3 pick a year earlier. It hardly worked out that way.

At first, Millen looked like a genius. Rogers was the first Lions rookie to score a pair of touchdowns in his first game. He had 22 catches for 243 yards in his first five games, averaging 11 yards per catch. Then while practicing a speed drill with Dre Bly, he broke his collarbone and was done for the season.

The collarbone was fine, and he was ready to go for the 2004 season. He got started on his off-season work early. He was a regular in the gym. Then he broke the same collarbone on the third play of that 2004 season and again was out for the year.

Instead of keeping Rogers around the facility to help him get over the injury physically and mentally, the Lions left him on his own. Looking back, it was a huge mistake by Millen.

Rogers, who had signed a six-year, $55 million contract, went back to smoking marijuana, which he admitted in an ESPN story by Jemele Hill. He told her he was leading the "Lamborghini" life.

It was a lifestyle that didn't mesh well with the NFL, which is basically a year-round job. When not playing the players have to stay in shape and remain sharp.

When Rogers showed up for training camp in 2005, the Lions saw that his lifestyle had caught up with him. He was slower, and while just a year previously he had been cast as a gym rat, now he just did the minimum. This wasn't lost on the Lions who drafted receiver Roy Williams in the first round with the intention of making him their top wide receiver.

After Rogers tested positive for marijuana three times, the NFL suspended him for five games. The Lions gave up on him and cut him in September 2006. In three seasons Rogers had played in just 15 games with 440 yards and four touchdowns (remember two came in his first game). Rogers had not learned his lesson. He added Vicodin to his daily routine. He drank heavily.

Every now and then throughout the years, his name appears in the news when he's been stopped or found (once in an On The Border restaurant in Novi) with a blood alcohol level above the legal limit.

The Lions moved on—an NFL team can do that. Yet Rogers remains one of the biggest draft failures, if not the biggest, in franchise history.

24 Russ Thomas Made His Mark

Russ Thomas was not particularly loved by Lions fans. There is some debate among the Lions faithful about who was the worst general manager—Thomas or Matt Millen.

For Thomas it had less to do with his curmudgeonly reputation than it did his record for 23 years as the team's general manager. In that stretch the Lions had only six winning seasons. During his regime the Lions made the playoffs just three times—in 1970, in 1982 (with a losing record during a strike season), and in 1983.

Thomas was held in high regard by his NFL associates, but the love didn't translate to the long-suffering fans who saw him as stingy and too tight with William Clay Ford's money.

For Thomas, the Lions were his life. It started when he was drafted out of Ohio State by Detroit in 1946. A knee injury in 1949 ended his playing career and was the reason he always walked with a limp. He may have been done playing, but he was just starting what would be a 42-year relationship with the Lions. He worked as a scout, broadcaster, assistant coach, controller, personnel director, and general manager.

He negotiated player contracts from 1967–89 when he was nudged out of the job by William Clay Ford, who had put him in charge of player personnel when he bought the Lions in 1964. Thomas wanted to stay on, but it was time or past time to go. He died in his sleep a few years later, in 1991, at his home in Naples, Florida. He was 66.

Thomas couldn't be appreciated until someone got close enough to get to know him. Charlie Sanders, Lions Hall of Fame tight end, was one of those who knew him well. Sanders went to Thomas after a business venture Sanders was involved in failed

Sanders told Thomas he was going to have to apply for workers compensation. Thomas approved it without hesitation. It was around Christmas time and Thomas literally emptied his pockets of all his cash so Sanders' children could have presents.

When Thomas died, Sanders said, "Everything he did was about winning. He wanted to win more than anybody I will ever know."

Thomas also gave a young man named Dan Jaroshewich a chance and a job. Jaroshewich was looking for part-time work in 1973. Thomas sat him down and told him to learn under equipment manager Roy "Friday" Macklem but staying would depend on him getting a college degree. So it was arranged that Jaroshewich could work during the season and work on his studies in the off-season.

For some people, Russ Thomas' door was always open.

Thomas got along well with coach Wayne Fontes and stood behind him after his 1987 accident when he was charged with driving under the influence and possession of cocaine. The drug charges were later dropped. Fontes said he got along with Thomas from Day 1.

Mike O'Hara, who covered the Lions as a beat writer for the *Detroit News*, once wrote that Thomas was consistent with the media—consistently stormy. He didn't much care what people thought of him.

Thomas is credited with the team's move from Tiger Stadium to the Silverdome in Pontiac. Also, the respect he had from his peers helped him get Super Bowl XVI to the Silverdome.

"He gave most of his life to the Lions and left an indelible mark on our organization," William Clay Ford said after Thomas' death. "Aside from our business relationship, Russ was a very dear personal friend."

25 Suh Does The Stomp

Ndamukong Suh's sophomore season will be remembered for The Stomp. It's too bad because there was much more to it than that. But The Stomp was a pivotal moment in Suh's second season as a starting defensive tackle for the Lions.

In the 2011 Thanksgiving game at Ford Field against the Green Bay Packers, Suh got tangled up with guard Evan Dietrich-Smith. When Suh stood up, he stomped on Dietrich-Smith's right arm after grinding his helmet into the turf. Replay after replay showed that clearly he made the stomp as an exclamation point.

The officials saw it and kicked Suh out of the game. Immediately afterward Suh spoke to the media. He did not offer an apology of any sort. Instead he said he was trying to extract himself from a situation. Not even the most gullible reporter was buying that line. We had seen replays of The Stomp.

His linemate, veteran Corey Williams, said he was going to talk to Suh about controlling his emotions on the field. Twenty-four hours later, Suh issued an apology to fans through a message on Facebook.

Suh then had a talk with NFL officials who suspended him for two games. They announced it was his fifth infraction of on-field rules that had resulted in league discipline with fines totaling $42,500. In other words, it was time for Suh to sit and think about it.

His previous fines included slamming the Browns' Jake Delhomme to the ground (August 28, 2010), giving the Bears' Jay Cutler a forearm to the back of the head (December 5, 2010), and slamming the Bengals' Andy Dalton to the ground by his head (August 12, 2011).

Suh is no friend of NFL quarterbacks. And vice-versa.

An appeal of his suspension was denied two days prior to the first game he missed and that same night he was in a car accident in Portland, Oregon, his hometown. He had driven his classic Chevy into a tree and water fountain. Alcohol was not involved. Still, on top of the suspension, the accident didn't do much to improve his image. Clearly it was tarnished.

As a rookie, Suh made an immediate impact on the NFL. Defensive rookie of the year plus a trip to the Pro Bowl—it was all part of the fun. As a defensive tackle Suh anchored a line that was expected to be the strength of the defense.

He was a force. But Suh drew the eyes of the officials, too. His explanation was that the NFL had never seen a player like him.

Early in his sophomore season, Suh arranged to meet with the NFL commissioner. He brought along coach Jim Schwartz and team president Tom Lewand. This was weeks before the suspension so obviously there was a gap in communication, or Suh let his emotions get the best of him.

Gunther May Say Anything

All reporters want is a coach who is straight-forward, readily available, and who can come up with quotes that are true gems. They got all of that in Gunther Cunningham, the defensive coordinator who was brought to Detroit in 2009 when Jim Schwartz was hired as head coach.

Cunningham, who is in his mid-60s, makes fun of his age and Schwartz joins right in. But nothing seems to pass by Cunningham. He fully embraced technological advances by using iPads to watch film and for use as a playbook.

"Some players don't want to come near me because of the way I talk. I'm liable to say anything," Cunningham said.

Players call him tough as nails and generally seem to appreciate him and his knowledge of the game. While he has been defensive coordinator, he can often be seen before or after practice on the field, chatting with some of his favorite offensive players.

After the meeting, a statement released by commissioner Roger Goodell's office said, "Ndamukong plays the game with great skill and passion and is a major reason for the Lions' success this year. In the course of our dialogue today, we reviewed video showing that Ndamukong has clearly made the adjustments to play consistently within the rules so that he can continue to help the team." Suh was not the same player in his second season. Before his suspension for the December 4 and 11 games, he had three sacks. Afterward he had just one. He had a team-high 10 sacks as a rookie, but his tackle numbers were down dramatically—he had 66 as a rookie and 36 in his second season.

Schwartz defended him. Statistics can be misleading, yet it was clear there was no stepping up. However, there was The Stomp.

26 Five Starters in 44 Days

It's easy for a winning team to attract free agents, but for a long unhealthy stretch starting in 2001, it was not easy at all for the Lions. Dollars are important, but winning is key. No one wants to move to the town of a perennial loser.

General Manager Martin Mayhew understood the predicament. Instead of using it as another excuse for futility, he worked around it. With the Lions coming off a 2–14 season in 2009, the first under coach Jim Schwartz, Mayhew put on his trading cap.

In 44 days in the spring of 2010, Mayhew made trades that netted the Lions five quality starters: defensive tackle Corey Williams, cornerback Chris Houston, backup quarterback Shaun Hill, left guard Rob Sims, and tight end Tony Scheffler.

Not a bad haul.

It all started when they got Williams and a seventh-round 2010 draft choice from Cleveland for a fifth-round 2010 pick on March 6, 2010. A week later Detroit got Houston from Atlanta for a 2010 sixth-round and a 2011 seventh-round pick.

Houston had grown out of favor with the Falcons, but a new city and new life proved that Mayhew knows defensive back talent. Of course, Mayhew was once an NFL cornerback, which also helped.

Houston developed under the tutelage of defensive coordinator Gunther Cunningham. Cornerback had been a weakness of the Lions for season after season, but Houston changed that scenario.

On March 16, Hill was acquired from San Francisco for a seventh-round pick in 2011. Hill was a perfect complement to Matthew Stafford who was entering his second season.

Hill had been a starter with the 49ers but lost the job to Alex Smith. Like every good quarterback, Hill wants to be a starter. But he totally understood his role upon arriving in Detroit and made the best of it. He could help the young Stafford learn the ways of the NFL. As an ultimate professional, Hill was ready to step in when needed. He started 10 games in the 2010 season when Stafford was out with shoulder injuries, going 3–7.

After those three deals, Mayhew was still just getting started. On April 6, the Lions filled a need on the offense, getting left guard Rob Sims and a seventh-round pick from Seattle in exchange for DE Robert Henderson and a 2010 fifth-round pick.

Not only did they get Sims in the deal, but they drafted defensive end Willie Young with that seventh-round pick. Young was a bit raw and didn't really adapt well in his rookie season. But he turned it around in his second season when he played regularly, rotating in at defensive end. Such a bonus.

Sims stepped in at starting left guard, a position that had been a revolving door for years and fit right in between left tackle Jeff Backus and center Dominic Raiola. Not only that but Sims is a

Midwesterner. Not that he didn't like Seattle, but he prefers football to coffee, so Detroit was a good fit.

One more trade completed that 44-day stretch. From Denver, the Lions acquired tight end Tony Scheffler, a Michigan native who grew up as a Lions' fan, in a three-team deal that sent linebacker Ernie Sims to Philadelphia.

Scheffler, who had played at Western Michigan, was thrilled to move back to his home state. Along with Brandon Pettigrew and Will Heller, tight end became a position of strength. In the 2011 season, Scheffler got out his dancing shoes. When he scored touchdowns—a career-high half-dozen—he would do a little end zone dance themed to the opponent.

Mayhew obtained five quality starters without giving up much other than draft picks. He was on his way to totally revamping the roster without over-paying free agents just to get them to town.

27 Are You Ready for Monday Night Football?

Only the best NFL teams play on the national stage that is *Monday Night Football*. That means the Lions haven't seen much air time on Monday nights in recent years. In fact there was a 10-year gap of no Monday night appearances starting in October 2001.

The Lions came roaring back on October 10, 2011, when they faced the Chicago Bears in a classic NFL North matchup. From the day the 2011 schedule was released, that Monday night was circled on the schedule. The Lions wanted to show the rest of the country they were not the same old Lions.

They went into the game with a 4–0 start to the season, feeling good but not too cocky. The Lions hadn't won a Monday night

A Lions fan holds up a sign that states, "ESPN Monday Night Football, Back in the Lions D" during a Week 5 game against the Chicago Bears on Monday, October 10, 2011, in Detroit, Michigan. The Lions won the game 24-13 to open the season with a 5-0 record. (AP Photo/Paul Spinelli)

game since September 28, 1998. The best way to get invited back is to win. And so the Lions did, and the fans helped.

The Ford Field crowd of 67,861 was the most fans ever at a Lions game at Ford Field. Only Super Bowl XL put more behinds in the Ford Field seats (68,206). And they were so loud that the Bears were whistled for nine false starts.

Running back Jahvid Best had a career-best 163 rushing yards, averaging 13.6 yards per carry, including a scamper of 88 yards. The run game was crucial late in the game to keep the Bears' offense on the sideline. The Lions had a 21–10 lead to start the fourth. Best had 54 rushing yards in the fourth quarter including a 43-yard run.

Matthew Stafford (19-of-26, 219 yards, two touchdowns, one interception) connected with Calvin Johnson for a 73-yard touchdown play. Johnson became the first player in NFL history to score nine touchdown receptions in the first five games of the season.

The Bears held a 10–7 half-time lead, but the Lions had earned the name Comeback Cats for recovering from much larger deficits.

With the win, the Lions snapped a five-game losing streak against the Bears. Detroit's last win against the Bears had been on October 28, 2007, when the Lions won 16–7 at Soldier Field. This was the fifth Monday night meeting for the Lions and Bears. The Lions are 4–1 in those match-ups.

It wasn't the biggest Monday night win in Lions' history, but it was important for a team trying to make a turn-around. The win gave them a 5–0 record to start the season. They gave a game ball

Ford Field Goes Purple

For the Lions' first nine years playing at Ford Field, they just weren't good enough to be scheduled for *Monday Night Football*. That didn't change until 2011.

But in 2010 Ford Field hosted a Monday night game on December 13. The Lions didn't play, however, it was a Giants and Vikings game. After snow collapsed the roof of the Minneapolis Metrodome two days earlier, the NFL went into emergency mode. Lions president Tom Lewand agreed to host the game in a very last-minute arrangement. Soon after the Lions played that Sunday, the field was changed because this was to be a home game for the Vikings. Some Ford Field and Lions employees got no sleep that night.

The purple paint in the on-field logos was barely dry at kickoff. The Vikings brought their loud horn that sounds at every score and even their mascot and cheerleaders.

The Lions didn't make money that night, but they were reimbursed for their expenses and earned Brownie points from the NFL offices.

to the fans who had caused the nine false starts with their volume. With the win the Lions drove up their *Monday Night Football* record to 12–13–1.

Another milestone Monday night game was an overtime win at Dallas on September 19, 1994. The Lions had lost four straight Monday night games. The Cowboys, who had won back-to-back Super Bowls, were heavily favored over the Lions who were 1–1 going into the contest.

It was billed as a contest between running backs Barry Sanders and Emmitt Smith, and they delivered. Sanders carried the ball 40 times for 194 yards, while Smith gained 192 yards on 29 carries and seven catches.

The Lions held a 17–7 lead, but the Cowboys, led by Troy Aikman, came back to tie it. Jason Hanson won it in overtime for the Lions with a 44-yard field goal.

The Lions finished that 1994 season 9–7 and sent five players to the Pro Bowl: Barry Sanders, Lomas Brown, Mel Gray, Herman Moore, and Chris Spielman.

28 Mike Utley Full of Life

While Mike Utley lost the use of his legs on the football field, he never lost his sense of adventure. He was always ready for a challenge. A wheelchair is no match for Utley.

A year or so after his accident on November 17, 1991, which paralyzed him from the chest down, he talked to Lions reporters about his next move. He was going to try sky-diving.

Really.

One reporter (actually, it was me) apologized for being indelicate and then asked the question everyone wanted to know. How exactly was he planning to land?

He took his hand and smacked it down on the table in front of him and said, "Splat."

Okay, then.

Utley, a 6'6", 290-pound guard, was drafted by the Lions in the third round (59th overall) in 1989 out of Washington State. He became the starting right guard as a rookie.

In his third season with the Lions in a game against the Los Angeles Rams, he fractured his sixth and seventh cervical vertebrae and suffered an extensive soft-tissue injury as he was pass-blocking on the first play of the fourth quarter of a 21–10 Lions win. He was 25 years old at the time.

Down on the turf at the Silverdome, he was taken off on a stretcher and underwent surgery at Henry Ford Hospital in Detroit. It wasn't known for 48 hours following surgery whether he would walk again.

As he was being rolled off the field, he gave the thumbs-up sign, which would come to represent his fighting spirit. His goal remains to walk unassisted off of Ford Field. As he says, "A man walks on the field of battle, and he walks off the field of battle."

The Lions won the game that day to move to 7–4. Then with Utley on their minds and in their hearts, the rest of the season was dedicated to him. The Lions reeled off five straight wins to finish the season 12–4. And then they went on to beat Dallas 38–6 in the first round of the playoffs. A week later their season ended with a 41–10 playoff loss at Washington.

Utley was a rock star sort of player with long hair that remains his style today.

Just nine weeks after his accident, on Super Bowl Sunday, he snuck out of Denver's Craig Hospital, the country's leading spinal-cord rehab center, to go to a 7–11 and get a beer. With a little help, he succeeded. Of course he did.

Utley still visits the Lions regularly, he's still part of the family even though he hasn't played for 20 years. He established The Mike Utley Foundation in 1992 to financially support research, rehabilitation, and education for others living with this disability.

Their goal, "Our mission is to shepherd an effective function-restoring treatment for spinal-cord injuries, to encourage through education that of adopting a rehabilitative lifestyle for the spinal-cord injured, and a public awareness of spinal-cord injuries."

Utley continues to work out religiously and work on physical therapy.

Photos on the website for the Mike Utley Foundation, represented by a thumbs-up logo, show him scuba diving, riding a wave runner, and skiing on a special apparatus. For more information on his foundation, see MikeUtley.org.

The former All-American has won a host of courage awards including the Detroit Lions Courage House–Ricky Sandoval Award in 2009.

29 Fontes, A Man With a Smile

Wayne Fontes enjoys the heck out of life. He loved being the Lions head coach, and he was good at it. Even after he was fired, he stayed true to the Honolulu blue.

When a group of reporters pulled up to the stadium in Tampa for the Lions playoff game in 1997, the season after Fontes was fired, the first familiar face they saw was Fontes in the parking lot with a cigar in one hand, a beverage in the other, and the patented Fontes smile.

Coach of the Year

Wayne Fontes is the Lions' winningest coach with 67 wins and the team's losingest coach with 71 losses. Midway through his nine-year tenure—in 1991—he was named NFL Coach of the Year by eight different groups. They include the Associated Press; the Maxwell Club; the Paul Brown Award by TD Club of Columbus, Ohio; Starter; United Press International; Football News; Pro Football Weekly; and Pro Football Writers Association.

In 2010, when the Lions finally broke their NFL record road losing streak at Tampa, Fontes was invited into the locker room by Coach Jim Schwartz afterward. Fontes still loved his Lions, and from all accounts the players got a kick out of him.

In his eight-plus seasons Fontes became the franchise's all-time winningest coach with a 67–71 record, including playoffs. Because of his longevity, he also lost more games than any Lions' head coach.

His job was made a little easier because he had Barry Sanders at running back, but of course there was more to it than that.

Fontes wasn't one of those coaches who sleeps at the office or burns the midnight oil. He did what he thought it took to get the job done. At practice Fontes was driven around in a golf cart, keeping an eye on everything. (I can't remember if he had a cigar during practice, but surely he didn't.)

In 1988, he was promoted from defensive coordinator with the Lions to interim head coach after Darryl Rogers was fired. Fontes was known as a players coach who excelled at motivation.

Fontes, a former high school football and basketball coach who played at Michigan State, propelled the Lions to the playoffs in 1991, 1993, 1994, and 1995. In 1991, they set a franchise record with 12 wins, and in 1993 they won the NFC Central Division title. In the playoffs after the 1991 season, the Lions won at home against Dallas. Through the 2011 season, it stood as the only Lions playoff win since 1957.

It wasn't all smiles for Fontes. Despite getting his Lions to the playoffs, they couldn't get to the next step, and after 1991 they didn't win a playoff game. Fontes was fired after the Lions finished the 1996 season with a 5–11 record. In 1995, they had featured one of the NFL's top offenses, but they didn't live up to expectations in 1996. Barry Sanders was close to Fontes, and there were rumors that he would leave when Fontes did, but Sanders stuck around a few more years.

Fontes moved back to the Tampa area and never coached again. It's not unusual to see him around when the Lions are in Tampa, however. He has a certain loyalty to the team that stuck with him for so many years.

In fact, when he was the defensive coordinator he got in some legal trouble. He was pulled over on suspicion on drunken driving in Rochester Hills near Oakland University. He had driven his car into a ditch before his wife brought him a second car. When he was pulled over, police found cocaine in the glove box. Fontes said it belonged to his son. The incident earned him the nickname "Cocaine Wayne." The drug charges were eventually dropped.

The guy with the big heart, Fontes was also good to others. One time he donned Mickey Mouse ears to promote a charity event. A Detroit newspaper ran the photo of Fontes wearing those mouse ears with a caption contest. Fontes was not amused.

30 Moore a Fan Favorite

After two seasons of languishing in Bobby Ross' offense, Herman Moore was excited, and he couldn't wait for the 2001 season to get started. To celebrate, the Pro Bowl wide receiver bought a

Herman Moore (84) during the NFL Pro Bowl, a 26–23 AFC overtime victory on February 2, 1997, at Aloha Stadium in Honolulu, Hawaii.
(AP Photo/NFL Photos)

Ferrari 360 Modena, a $200,000 machine. Moore went for the "fly yellow" color because it looked like it was going fast even when sitting idle. A car buff, Moore had previously owned a Ferrari Testarossa, a Lamborghini Diablo, four Jaguars, and two Porsches.

Now Moore felt he was getting a new lease on his career as a key element in Marty Mornhinweg's West Coast offense, and he wanted to arrive in style. Too bad it didn't work out.

Moore injured his hip in the 2001 season. He thought he was ready to play two weeks later, but he'd already been placed on Injured Reserve, a controversial move, which ended his season.

Moore, who wore No. 84, was always a favorite in Detroit. He stood tall, had great mitts, worked hard, and loved a little of the spotlight. If he hadn't been a wide receiver, he might have tried for an acting career. A movie buff, when he built a new home during his playing days it was complete with a movie theater. Moore and his colleague Johnnie Morton even had bit roles in the movie *Jerry Maguire*.

Moore faded out in his final three seasons, rounding out his 11-year NFL career after being drafted in the first round (10th overall) out of Virginia in 1991. He arrived in Detroit with high

Herman Moore's Best Games

It should be no surprise that three of wide receiver Herman Moore's best games came in the 1995 season when the Lions' offense set the NFL on fire. In his career, Moore only had one game with three touchdown catches on October 29, 1995, in a win over Green Bay. Here are his top five games based on yardage:

1. December 4, 1995—183 yards, 14 receptions, 1 TD
2. November 5, 1995—176 yards, 9 catches, 0 TDs
3. November 24, 1994—169 yards, 7 catches, 1 TD
4. September 1, 1996—157 yards, 12 catches, 1 TD
5. November 6, 1994—151 yards, 8 catches, 2 TDs

expectations. He didn't disappoint. His rookie season was a thrill. While Moore was trying to fit in, the Lions won their first playoff game and were just one win away from playing in the Super Bowl. He was named to the Pro Bowl four times and was voted to the first team All-Pro team three times.

Moore hit his peak with Scott Mitchell at quarterback from 1995–97. In those seasons he had 123 catches for 1,686 yards, 106 receptions for 1,296 yards, and 104 catches for 1,293 yards, respectively. The Lions went to the playoffs in two of those seasons—1995 and 1997.

Despite an assault on the receiving records by Calvin Johnson in the 2011 season, Moore's franchise record of 1,686 receiving yards in a season still stands. Johnson came up five yards short.

Moore also still holds the records for most receptions in a season (123), career receiving touchdowns (62), career receptions (670), career receiving yards (9,174), career 100-yard receiving games (35), and 100-yard receiving games in a season (10).

He's also tied with Calvin Johnson for most games in a season with two-plus receiving touchdowns. While not a record of any sorts, it is amazing that he fumbled just five times and lost four of those when you consider how often Moore touched the ball. That's in his entire Lions' career.

Moore's career went a bit south after Scott Mitchell was let go following the 1998 season. Like Matthew Stafford and Calvin Johnson, the two had good communication. Mitchell knew what Moore was going to do and vice-versa.

Moore was injured during the 1999 season, playing just eight games with 16 total catches that season. In 2000 Bobby Ross gave the starting job to Germane Crowell.

After 11 seasons in Detroit, Moore signed with the New York Giants but played just one game with no stats. He was done.

It's a funny thing—after all his success as a wide receiver, Moore had started out on defense at the University of Virginia. In the second week of the preseason of his freshman year, the coaches decided he was useless at safety and moved him to wide receiver.

When he left Virginia, he had a school record 27 touchdown catches and 2,504 receiving yards.

31 Best Seventh-Round Pick Ever?

Joe Schmidt was injury-ridden during his college years at Pittsburgh, which didn't put him too high on the Lions' draft board in 1953. He was also only 6' tall, but they didn't measure the size of his heart. Detroit waited to draft him until the seventh round.

Nice move.

In his 13 seasons with the Lions, Schmidt was stellar. He was named NFL Defensive Player of the Year four times. He was a team captain nine years. In 1999, *The Sporting News* ranked him 65th on the list of 100 greatest football players of all time. In 1969, he was voted the Greatest Lion Ever in conjunction with the NFL's 50th anniversary.

Schmidt was voted to the NFL all-league team 10 times. He was elected to the Pro Bowl 10 straight years from 1955–64, and his teammates voted him their Most Valuable Player four times.

Best seventh-round pick ever? Quite possibly.

Schmidt, a linebacker, stepped in during his rookie season and helped the Lions win their second straight NFL championship. They won another two during his tenure.

He developed the middle linebacker position, which was fairly new in the 1950s as teams started using a 4-3 front. Schmidt could tackle well. He possessed the speed to evade a larger guard or to

A Vote for Roger Brown

While 18 former Detroit Lions have been enshrined in the Pro Football Hall of Fame, perhaps a few have been left out.

Joe Schmidt, former Lions linebacker and coach, thinks one of those should be his former teammate, Roger Brown. Brown was instrumental in the Lions' upset win over the Packers on Thanksgiving in 1962. He sacked quarterback Bart Starr six times that day.

"Roger should be in the Hall of Fame, but for some reason he's not. That particular day he was throwing those people around like toys," Schmidt said.

The Lions' defensive coordinator at the time was Don Shula.

Brown played for the Lions from 1960 through 1966 when he was traded to the Los Angeles Rams. While with the Lions he was named the 1962 Outstanding Defensive Lineman in the league. He set a record that year by sacking Starr and Johnny Unitas both for safeties in one season, an NFL record. He was a Pro Bowl player for six straight seasons (1962–67) and had the distinction of being the first NFL player to have a playing weight of more than 300 pounds. He played college ball at Maryland Eastern Shore and was inducted into the College Football Hall of Fame in 2009. He's now the owner of Roger Brown's Restaurant and Sports Bar in Portsmouth, Virginia.

drop back in coverage. He was also strong enough to get by would-be blockers.

What made Schmidt stand out was his ability to read offenses.

He played 13 seasons for the Lions, but there was a sticky moment before the 1958 season. In 1957, his salary was $11,000. After serving six months in the service in the off-season he was a holdout when training camp started. He and the Lions reached a deal, and that season he had six interceptions and set a new NFL record by recovering eight fumbles.

In 1962, along with four teammates, Schmidt admitted to betting on the 1962 NFL Championship Game between the Green Bay Packers and New York Giants. He was fined $2,000.

He announced his retirement as a player in March 1966 and was named an assistant coach. That didn't last long—just a year—because when coach Harry Gilmer was let go after much conflict with his players, Schmidt was named head coach.

Schmidt established curfews, traded unhappy players, and finished his first season as head coach with a 5–7–2 record. In 1970, he guided the Lions to their first playoff appearance in 13 years. They lost 5–0 to Dallas. He resigned on January 12, 1973, saying that coaching wasn't fun anymore. During his tenure, he had built a 43–35–7 record.

As a nice farewell, three weeks after his resignation he was elected to the Pro Football Hall of Fame.

In an interview with the Hall of Fame, Schmidt said it was more difficult to be the coach than a player. He didn't have much coaching experience after just a year as an assistant, but his assistant coaches helped him. He was only 35 when he was named the head coach, which was young back in 1967 and would still be considered young today.

After leaving football, he became a manufacturer's rep, selling auto parts and working in that field until retirement. You can bet he had some good stories to tell.

32 Sims Hot From the Start

In Billy Sims' hometown of Hooks, Texas, there's a city street named Billy Sims Road. Their hometown son won the Heisman Trophy in 1978 at the University of Oklahoma where he played for Coach Barry Switzer. Sims was only the sixth junior to win the coveted trophy and was a runner-up in his senior season.

In Detroit, fans hardly got a chance to know the Heisman Trophy running back. The Lions drafted Sims with the first overall

Another No. 1

Everyone knows that between 1980 and 2009, the Lions had the No. 1 overall pick just twice. In 1980 they drafted running back Billy Sims, who is now in the Pro Football Hall of Fame. They got that one right. In 2009 they selected quarterback Matthew Stafford out of Georgia with the top pick. In just his third season, he threw for more than 5,000 yards—only three other quarterbacks in NFL history have reached that mark.

So prior to 1980, who were the Lions' No. 1 overall picks?

In 1950, it was Leon Hart who had played defensive end and tight end at Notre Dame. He was the only player to win the Heisman Trophy, a national championship, and be the first overall pick in the NFL draft all in the same one-year span—until Cam Newton accomplished it in 2011.

The only other No. 1 overall pick was running back Frank Sinkwich, who was drafted out of Georgia in 1943. He played for the Lions in 1943 and 1944 then he served in the United States Merchant Marines and the United States Army Air Force, but a knee injury received while playing for the 2nd Air Force service team in 1945 cut short his playing career that ended after two seasons in the All-America Football Conference. If it hadn't been for the war, Sinkwich might have had a longer career.

So it seems the Lions have drafted well when the most pressure is on.

---

pick in the 1980 draft. He got off to a terrific start with three rushing touchdowns (10 yards, 1 yard, 41 yards) in his first game as a rookie, a 41–20 win over the Los Angeles Rams at Anaheim Stadium. That day he had 22 carries for 153 yards and two catches for 64 yards, including a 60-yard pass play.

After that first game, the Lions' media relations phone didn't stop ringing. Sims was a hot topic, and he was sought out by *Sports Illustrated*, the *Chicago Tribune*, the *Washington Post* and the *New York Daily News*. He appeared on the cover of *Sports Illustrated* with the headline, "Pride of the Lions."

Bob Talbert, a popular *Detroit Free Press* columnist at the time, suggested that Billy Sims had all the credentials and tools to join

Billy Sims (20) leaps over New Orleans Saints tacklers in the fourth quarter on October 12, 1980, in Pontiac, Michigan. Simms scored on the play, and Detroit defeated New Orleans 24–13. (AP Photo/William Fundaro)

Alan Trammell and Thomas Hearns as Detroit's new heroes of the 1980s. Before Sims was drafted, there was some debate among fans whether the Lions should draft Sims or the 1979 Heisman Trophy winner Charles White out of USC.

If you compare the first NFL games of Sims and White, it's easy to see that the Lions made the right choice. In his first game,

White had just two yards on four carries and caught three passes for no gain for the Cleveland Browns who had drafted him. White's career was short-lived, but that was due to cocaine, not an injury. In four seasons in Cleveland, White accumulated just 942 yards before playing four years for the Rams, including his only 1,000-yard season in 1987.

Sims was named to the Pro Bowl in his first three seasons.

He led the Lions to the playoffs in 1982 and 1983 but, of course, they didn't win. The most disappointing playoff loss was in 1983, a wild-card game at San Francisco, when Sims ran for 114 yards on 20 carries. Joe Montana led the 49ers to a comeback victory, and Eddie Murray missed a field goal in the final seconds.

The Lions have faced many heart-breaking injuries over the years. Count Sims as one of those. In 1984, his fifth NFL season, he suffered a catastrophic knee injury in a game against the Minnesota Vikings. His career was over.

His impressive career stats read 1,131 carries for 5,106 yards (4.5 yards per carry) and 186 receptions for 2,072 yards (11.1 yards per catch).

He wore No. 20, and five years after Sims' career was over, another Heisman Trophy winner took it over—Barry Sanders. It was also the same number worn by Hall of Fame defensive back Lem Barney.

Following his retirement from the NFL, Sims had a series of bad business deals and questionable investments. He filed for bankruptcy in 1990.

In 2007 a bronze statue of Sims was dedicated at Heisman Park at the University of Oklahoma to commemorate his 1978 award.

In 2008 during Sam Bradford's Heisman Trophy acceptance speech, Sims yelled out, "Boomer, Sooner," embarrassing himself and nearly everyone else. He deflected the spotlight off Bradford who was undergoing a life-changing event. Sims later apologized.

33 Back-to-Back Titles

No matter the era, no matter the sport, it's tough to win back-to-back championships. But no one told the 1953 Lions that they couldn't do it. They had beaten Cleveland in 1952 for their first title since 1935. The Lions went back to the championship game a year later.

Jim Doran caught one touchdown pass for the Lions in the 1953 season. He made it count. With more than two minutes left in the game at Briggs Stadium (later known as Tiger Stadium), Doran caught a 33-yard touchdown pass from quarterback Bobby Layne.

Doak Walker kicked the extra point to give the Lions the 17–16 win over the Cleveland Browns in a come-from-behind victory to seal their second-straight world professional football title on December 27, 1953. They did it in front of 54,577 fans.

The Lions became the third team ever to win back-to-back championship games. They had done it two years in a row over the Browns. The previous year the Lions had prevailed 17–7.

"Our Lions Are Still Kings" was the headline in the *Detroit Free Press* the next day.

Many of the same names on both rosters had battled it out the year before. Perhaps none had a worse day than Browns quarterback "Automatic" Otto Graham who was just 2-of-15 passing for 20 yards. It was his worst day in eight years of professional football.

Lou "The Toe" Groza had kicked three Browns field goals—a pair in the fourth quarter—to give the Browns a 16–10 edge with less than five minutes remaining. With 4:00 left and the Lions trailing 16–10, they had the ball on their own 20. Using exactly two minutes and four passes—the final one being the touchdown to Doran—they scored.

After Doran's touchdown, with 2:08 left, the Browns got the football back. The game wasn't over. But then rookie halfback Carl Karilivacz intercepted Graham on his first pass play. The Lions got the ball back and were able to run down the clock.

It wasn't a pretty game. Newspaper accounts said it was marked by "flying fists that embroiled virtually every member of both squads." Twenty of the 33 points scored were a result of interceptions or fumbles.

For their efforts, the winning Lions each received $2,424.10. Pay was based on a formula that involved gate receipts and subtracted travel costs. It was a good pay day at a time when many of the players worked 9-to-5 jobs in the off-season.

The television blackout rules were different back then. Even though the game was sold out, the championship game (the Super Bowl of its era) was not televised locally, but it could be seen outside of the metro area and in cities around the state. Many fans were forced to hop in their cars and drive to Brighton or beyond to be able to watch their beloved Lions beat the Browns for the second straight year for their second straight championship.

Most of them would have probably agreed it was worth the trip.

The next week the game was televised in its entirety on one of the Detroit stations. My, how far we've come and how far we have to go. A sell-out these days lifts the TV blackout. And Lions fans can only dream of winning one championship, let alone two straight.

34 Out on a Winning Note

So long, Pontiac. After 26 seasons of calling the Pontiac Silverdome home, the Lions played their final game there on January 6, 2002. The Lions went out on a high note with a 15–10 win over the Dallas Cowboys. It was Detroit's second win of the season.

The ever-loyal diehard Lions fans were into it. In the fourth quarter the Cowboys were driving for a potential go-ahead touchdown. The crowd noise was so loud that Dallas was penalized two times for false starts. It was meant to be the Lions' day.

Coach Marty Mornhinweg fired his hat and jacket into the crowd. The players did a victory lap, high-fiving fans who were so excited that wide receiver Johnnie Morton said they almost tore off his arm.

It was the first win for quarterback Ty Detmer, who threw a 20-yard pass to tight end David Sloan in the second quarter. A two-point conversion failed.

Dallas running back Emmitt Smith had scored on a 2-yard run in the second to give Dallas the early lead. Detroit was down 7–6 at the half, but Jason Hanson kicked a 47-yard field goal, then Dallas' Jon Hilbert sailed one between the goal posts to give Dallas a 10–9 lead.

In the fourth quarter, Johnnie Morton caught a 16-yard pass from Detmer but again the two-point conversion failed. Still the Lions had a 15–10 lead, and it held thanks to the vociferous fans.

Afterward police caught fans trying to take out "souvenirs" from the Silverdome. When it was all over, 25 to 30 seat backs were missing.

The Lions' relationship with the city of Pontiac, which owned and operated the Silverdome, had grown contentious after the team tried to work out a deal that would let them stay. So it was good riddance for the Lions who had built Ford Field, which was a brand-spanking new stadium in the heart of Detroit.

No souvenirs were sold commemorating the final day of the Lions at the Silverdome, which had originally cost $55.7 million to construct. Perhaps that's why fans got creative and tried to take their own.

That final win put the Lions' record at the Silverdome at 116–92–1, not including a 1–1 playoff mark. During 26 seasons only eight times did they finish with a winning record. Three seasons they hit the .500 mark.

Dome sweet Dome? Maybe not. Until FedEx Field opened in suburban Washington, D.C., the Silverdome was the largest NFL stadium, seating 80,311 for football. It made it a tough place to sell out to lift local television blackouts. Sometimes big is too big.

When the Lions built Ford Field, they downsized to a 65,000 seat capacity. When the team started winning, sell-outs were not an issue.

In 1975, the Silverdome was officially called the Pontiac Metropolitan Stadium. The first game was played with a partially open roof. The Lions beat the Kansas City Chiefs 27–24 in pre-season action.

Prior to moving to the Silverdome, the Lions had spent 36 seasons playing at Tiger Stadium (1938–74), which was once called Briggs Stadium.

The Silverdome was home to the Detroit Pistons from 1978–88 and hosted a variety of events. On December 31, 1975, Elvis Presley performed in his first New Year's Eve concert. The San Francisco 49ers topped the Cincinnati Bengals in Super Bowl XVI at the Silverdome on January 24, 1982.

The biggest crowd ever at the Silverdome was not there for a sporting event but to see Pope John Paul II celebrate Mass on September 18, 1987. He drew 93,682 followers.

35 Built with Character

When Ford Field was just a dream, there was a vision. Bill Ford Jr., the Lions' vice chairman, wanted the Lions' new home to be a unique building oozing with character. And, perhaps most importantly, when you stood on the 50-yard line, he wanted you to know you were in Detroit.

It wasn't as easy as it might sound. It took vision and perhaps a little luck. The mission was accomplished by incorporating the old J.L. Hudson warehouse into the plan. It wasn't the original plan, however.

A taxpayer referendum passed in November 1996, putting together the financing for a new stadium in downtown Detroit.

"We spent a good part of the rest of 1996 and most of 1997 looking at a stand-alone building. It was about early 1998 that we started to look at the aesthetics of the stand-alone building and the cost of the stand-alone building, it didn't feel right to us," said Lions president Tom Lewand, who has heavily involved in the stadium project.

"It looked like a lot of other stadiums that had been built or were being built. It didn't have enough of the unique characteristics that Mr. Ford and Bill [Ford Jr.] wanted us to have," Lewand said.

They were moving out of the Silverdome, which looked like the RCA Dome, which looked like the Carrier Dome. They had purchased the property, and the original design wasn't good enough, even on paper. "We tried to be different, but it looked like we were putting window dressing on something that was fundamentally similar to everything else," Lewand said.

In the early part of 1998, they challenged the designers to look at things differently. One of the ideas they came up with was utilizing the old J.L. Hudson warehouse.

Lucky for the foresight of Ford Jr., that warehouse was available. When the Lions bought the property for the stadium, the warehouse was just outside the footprint. At the time Ford wasn't sure what would become of it, but he decided to buy the warehouse because he thought they should own it.

"If it weren't for his foresight, none of that would have happened. We didn't know when Bill made the decision, would it be torn down and built into parking lot? Would it be a shopping mall? We didn't know," Lewand said. "Because it was there and because Bill had bought it, we were able to look at it as a means of incorporation into

Ford Field prior to the Minnesota Vikings–Detroit Lions game on Sunday, September 20, 2009. (AP Photo/Paul Sancya)

the building that accomplished both of the things that were elusive to us at that point—No. 1 the aesthetics and the unique qualities and characteristics, and No. 2 the cost. As the design evolved and it became a reality, Bill sold the building back to the project, and it all became part of the grander scheme of things."

He remembers at the ground-breaking—they used bulldozers, not a shovel—the renderings were first made public to good reviews. But there were skeptics who thought the finished stadium could never look like that. Even Lewand said it was hard to imagine when looking at the weed-strewn property full of dilapidated buildings before construction started.

Ford Field Up Close

Address: 2000 Brush St., Detroit

Capacity: 65,000

Number of suites: 132

Cost: $500 million

Construction schedule: 32 months

Completion date: August 2002

Sources of funding: City of Detroit, Detroit Downtown Development Authority, Wayne County, The Detroit Lions Inc., Ford Motor Company, Comerica Bank, and corporate funding investors.

Square feet of building: 1,826,250 (includes lease space)

Number of locker rooms: 11

Field surface: FieldTurf

Area of field level: 97,000 square feet

Events at Ford Field (with attendance): Super Bowl XL on February 5, 2006 (68,206); 2009 NCAA Final Four on April 4 and 6, 2009 (145,491); 2008 NCAA Midwest Regionals on March 28 and 30, 2008 (114,591); Basketbowl featuring Michigan State vs. Kentucky on December 13, 2003 (78,129); Wrestlemania 23 on April 1, 2007 (80,103); 2010 NCAA Frozen Four on April 8 and 10, 2010 (72,546).

"I remember one of the things that went through my mind when we were getting close to opening the building was how much it resembled the renderings that we had released in 1999, three years earlier," Lewand said.

He also remembers the day of the first game at Ford Field, a 2002 preseason contest with the Pittsburgh Steelers. Along with Bill Ford Jr., Lewand was standing on the club level overlooking the main atrium as people walked in and got their first look.

"I remember [Steelers wide receiver] Antwaan Randle El was on the field warming up, he was looking around, and he ran into the goal posts," Lewand said. "It was unlike anything else people had seen. Now you've got Lucas Oil Stadium [in Indianapolis], which, in the grand tradition of architecture, borrowed liberally from our building and we borrowed liberally from others.... There's a lot of great new stadiums, but the fundamental character of our building has remained the same since we opened in 2002."

36 Gridiron Heroes

It was a little difficult in the lean years to be the singer of the Detroit Lions fight song, "Gridiron Heroes."

Norah Duncan was the chosen one from 1998 to 2002 for games at the Silverdome. He once said he felt like the Maytag repairman—always ready to work but rarely called on. He did admit to enjoying the games, and he could bring guests and family, but he was done when the Lions moved to Ford Field for the 2002 season. Duncan said he found it easier to watch them lose on television. "I could always turn off the television," he said.

With the turn-around of the team, the fight song is once again being heard more often at Ford Field. Now it's with the vocal stylings of Theo "Gridiron" Spight, a loyal Lions fan. He's been known to show up at pregame tailgate parties to lead fans in a chorus or two, firing them up for the game.

The song itself has quite a history as one of the oldest fight songs in the NFL. When the Portsmouth Spartans moved to Detroit in 1934, owner G.A. Richards changed the name to the Lions to keep with the cat theme the baseball Tigers had started. Richards asked Graham Overgard, the Wayne State director of bands, to write a fight song.

It is sung after every score. What most fans don't know is that what's sung at the stadium is actually the chorus. The verse that proceeds it is rarely heard and has almost been forgotten.

(Verse)
Hail the colors Blue and Silver let them wave.
Sing their song and cheer the Gridiron Heroes brave,
Fighting for fame, winning the game,
Dashing to victory as they go.

(Chorus)
Forward down the field,
A charging team that will not yield.
And when the Blue and Silver wave,
Stand and cheer the brave.
Rah, rah, rah.
Go hard, win the game.
With honor you will keep your fame.
Down the field and gain,
A Lions victory!
GO LIONS!

Not a Pom-Pom Anywhere

Where are the cheerleaders? It's a question asked at least once a season. The short answer is that the Lions believe the most important entertainment they can provide on game day is between the lines on the field.

Back in the Silverdome days, they usually had cheerleaders from four area high schools who would rotate to the corners around the stadium, wearing their high school cheerleading uniforms.

A group of cheerleaders called the Detroit Pride was formed in 2010, but they are not official. They buy game tickets and cheer from the stands, but they can't get on the field.

Even though it's an old fight song, you could call it a classic, the Lions didn't always have someone to lead the fans in singing it. In 1993, they hired "Fat" Bob Taylor, the singing plumber, to do the honors. Duncan took over five years later.

It's a Lions' tradition that has made it through the lean seasons, not unlike thousands of diehard fans.

37 Emotions Rule the Day

Football is an emotional game but never more so than on December 21, 1997, in a Lions 13–10 win over the New York Jets.

It was the Lions' final game of the regular season, so it was the last chance for Barry Sanders to top the 2,000-yard rushing mark. He was 131 yards shy. It's difficult to imagine that Sanders became the secondary story that day. But he did.

In the fourth quarter, linebacker Reggie Brown went down and stayed down. He was assisting on a tackle of Jets halfback Adrian Murrell. In the collision his top two neck vertebrae were dislocated, bruising his spinal cord and leaving him unable to breathe and with no feeling below the neck.

He was motionless on the turf for nearly 20 minutes. He struggled to breathe, and his lips turned blue. A doctor gave mouth-to-mouth resuscitation on the field.

Even though the ambulance had been called, wide receivers Herman Moore and Johnnie Morton didn't know and became impatient. They thought the whole process was taking too long. So they ran to the tunnel, grabbed the gurney, and wheeled it out onto the turf.

The crowd had been quieted, and the scene of Moore and Morton doing their best to offer help put each fan a little more on edge.

Brown had suffered significant damage between the first and second vertebrae in his neck. He underwent fusion surgery, and the doctors said it would take 72 hours to know whether he could lead a relatively normal life.

His NFL career was over. He was 23 and had played 26 games after being drafted by the Lions 17th overall in the 1996 draft out of Texas A&M. Coach Bobby Ross said Brown was the best athlete on the team after Barry Sanders.

Three weeks later at a press conference, doctors praised the fast action of the Lions doctors and trainers immediately after the incident, crediting them with saving Brown's life.

And then as a surprise to all, Brown, wearing a halo neck brace, got up and walked to the podium. "When it first happened, I thought I'd never be able to walk again. It was a freak accident. I'm looking forward to getting back home and getting my life together," he said. He was able to lead a relatively normal life—minus football—with the addition of a vertical scar at the top of his neck.

Back to the other big story that day.

Sanders became just the third player in NFL history to top the 2,000-yard mark for one season. It wasn't easy. In his first eight carries he only accumulated 20 yards, but the Lions kept feeding the ball to him and he finished with 184 yards, his 14th straight 100-yard rushing game.

He hit 2,053 yards that day. He didn't have much to say afterward. The Lions win gave them a 9–7 record and a trip to the playoffs. Sanders accomplished his goal.

Immediately afterward, though, the main concern was Reggie Brown.

Reporters were emotionally spent. Not only had they seen Brown go down and Sanders run up the yards, but earlier in the game, directly below the press box, a fan had a heart attack. Medics were called, they moved the fan into the aisle, and used paddles to try to get his heart started. Eventually, he was carried down the aisle and onto the field into a waiting ambulance.

Before the writers left the press box that night, they were given word that the fan had died.

Emotions ruled the day and the night.

38 Disheartened Ross Leaves

Beat writers who approached the Silverdome on Monday morning after a hugely disappointing 23–8 loss to Miami the day before noticed something was different. The Jaguar belonging to team owner William Clay Ford Sr. was parked at the curb. That wasn't a typical sight on a Monday morning.

Something was up. It was November 6, 2000. Soon the rumors that filled the air became fact. Nine games into the season, five of them wins, Coach Bobby Ross quit. He had been on the verge of tears after the loss. His Lions had fallen behind 23–0 for the second straight game. At Indianapolis the previous week, his Lions had lost 30–18. Ross, in his fourth season in Detroit, had grown increasingly frustrated.

So that morning he informed his players and Ford that he was burned out by the task of trying to build a consistent winner. Actually, he had talked to Ford after the game on Sunday night to tell him he was leaving. But the longtime Lions' owner recommended that Ross sleep on it and get back to him in the morning. Ross did.

Ross issued a statement to Ford that said in part, "I am sorry, also, for not giving you the championship trophy you so richly deserved. Your strong support was my constant motivation."

Ross, who was 63, had been dealing with health issues, including blood clots. But perhaps it was the increasing mental errors and the lack of intensity by his team that sent him out the door.

He was a coach who beat everyone into the building and burned the midnight oil. Ross was known as "The General" due to his coaching stint at The Citadel (1973–77) and also because he was a taskmaster.

At one point during his tenure, his frustration rose so much after a penalty-filled loss that he made each player who had drawn a penalty run sprints. That included Pro Bowl defensive end Robert Porcher, who was not happy.

In that loss, the Lions turned over the ball three times—two fumbles and an interception by Stoney Case who stepped in after Charlie Batch was injured. Ross had been hired in January 1997 to replace Wayne Fontes, who had been the coach for a dozen years.

Ross had spent the previous five seasons in San Diego where he had brought the 1994 San Diego Chargers to an appearance in Super Bowl XXIX. Prior to that he had coached Georgia Tech to a share of the national championship.

Ross, who had one year remaining on his five-year deal with the Lions, finished his NFL career with a 77–68 record, including playoffs.

In 1997, his first season with the Lions, Ross coached them to a 9–7 record in the NFC Central and a wild-card playoff spot. They lost 20–10 at Tampa Bay with Scott Mitchell as the starting quarterback.

In 1998, the Lions finished a very disappointing 5–11 in what was to be Barry Sanders' last season. It was also Charlie Batch's first season as a starter.

In 1999, the Lions bounded back and an 8–8 record was good enough for an NFC wild-card berth. They lost 27–13 at the Washington Redskins in an ugly contest.

It didn't take long for Ford to find a replacement. Gary Moeller, the former University of Michigan coach, had been on Ross' staff and was promoted to assistant head coach prior to the 2000 season.

Moeller, who was the 10th coach under owner William Clay Ford, signed a three-year deal and was introduced that Monday morning as the next head coach.

After leaving the Lions, Ross took a three-year break from coaching. He then returned in 2004 as the head coach at Army, taking over a program that had gone 0–13 in 2003. In three years at Army, he improved their record to 9–25, up from their 4–32 performance during the three years prior to his arrival.

39 The Day the Music Died

Barry Sanders was always the quiet one. That didn't change when he stunned the city of Detroit and all Lions fans by abruptly retiring two days before the start of training camp in July 1999.

Sanders didn't face the media and would not even talk to Coach Bobby Ross about his decision to leave the Lions and the NFL.

Instead, he released a statement that was posted on the website of the *Wichita Eagle*. At the time Sanders lived in Wichita during the off-season.

It said, "My desire to exit the game is greater than my desire to remain in it. I have searched my heart through and through and feel comfortable with this decision."

While there had been hints that Sanders would leave the game, he still had four years remaining on a contract that he had signed just two years previously. Ross had been trying to contact Sanders since the season had ended, but Sanders didn't respond to his messages. He also skipped the required minicamps.

Uncharacteristically, the Lions had drafted a running back, Sedrick Irvin of Michigan State, in the fourth round of the draft just months before Sanders left. After the draft Ross said that it was difficult to know what Sanders was thinking. Sanders' agent said he had decided to retire in January but gave himself time to think it over.

Sanders' dad had almost become a joke around town because of his rambling that his son would never compare to James Brown.

After Sanders posted his retirement statement, an Associated Press reporter ran into Sanders at Heathrow Airport in London, England. Sanders told him he didn't say good-bye too well, and he wasn't a TV-camera type of person.

Barry Sanders' Five Worst Games

The franchise running back had a habit of running for short negative-yardage plays. Usually he broke enough long ones to compensate. But not always. Here are his lowest rushing yard games:

1. Minus–1 yard, 13 attempts—December 31, 1994 (playoffs)
2. 1 yard, 5 attempts—October 1, 1989
3. 10 yards, 12 attempts—October 28, 1990
4. 16 yards, 12 attempts—September 11, 1994
5. 20 yards, 10 attempts—September 7, 1997

There was much speculation about his real decision to leave. Sanders was such a competitor, and apparently he didn't see the situation in Detroit improving.

In his 10 years he had played in six playoff games, losing five of them.

Speculation was that he didn't like Bobby Ross, but in his autobiography, *Barry Sanders: Now You See Him*, Sanders said that Ross had nothing to do with his departure and he praised Ross as a head coach. He was upset that the Lions had released Pro Bowl center Kevin Glover, a good friend of his, for salary cap reasons.

He also put the Lions in a bind. With training camp imminent, they were missing a key element of their offense.

So they acquired running back Greg Hill in a trade that sent two draft picks to St. Louis. Hill started eight games in 1999 and rushed for 542 yards and two touchdowns. He was released by the Lions after that season.

After Sanders' unexpected retirement, the Lions demanded he return a portion of his $11 million signing bonus. Sanders refused, the Lions sued, and the team won a judgment against him.

Many Lions fans were irate. He was their hope. After 10 years, he was the Lions. He alone was worth the price of admission. He had rushed for 15,269 yards during those 10 years. He needed just 1,458 yards to pass Walter Payton's mark for the best all-time.

No one had the chance to say good-bye to No. 20. He never gave them the chance. They thought he owed them that. For many years, even today, there are fans who have not forgiven him.

Time heals all wounds, and slowly Sanders is making his way back into the Lions' family. He did the intro for the October 2011 *Monday Night Football* game. He attended the game and received a huge round of applause.

Slowly and quietly, he has worked his way back into the hearts of Lions fans.

40 From Portsmouth to Detroit

It was the third time Detroit had entered the National Football League, but in 1934 it stuck.

Something connected with the city of Detroit and the Lions. George A. Richards headed a group that purchased the Portsmouth (Ohio) Spartans for $7,952.08 and moved them to Detroit on June 30, 1934. Coach George "Potsy" Clark, who had coached the previous two years in Portsmouth, made the trip to Detroit to continue coaching the team.

They were a running team, these 1934 Lions. In their first-ever game in Detroit, the Lions beat the New York Giants 9–0 at the University of Detroit Stadium in front of 12,000 fans on September 23, 1934. That day they ran the ball for 185 yards and passed for just two. Whatever works.

Lions quarterback Earl "Dutch" Clark obviously had to do more than pass, he could carry the ball, as well. He could also kick. There was no score until late in the third quarter when Clark drop-kicked a field goal after eight rushing first downs. The Lions were up 3–0.

Then with a half minute to play, the Giants took a final chance with a Hail Mary pass attempt, but it was intercepted by halfback Roy "Father" Lumpkin who ran it 60 yards down the right sideline for a touchdown as time ran out.

It was the first of seven straight shutouts and 10 straight wins for the Lions. They lost their first game 3–0 on November 25 to Green Bay.

They not only moved to Detroit that year, but they also started the Thanksgiving tradition that has continued throughout the years. On November 29, they played their first Thanksgiving home game and lost 19–16 to the undefeated defending World Champion Chicago Bears before a crowd of 26,000.

In previous incarnations the Detroit NFL teams had been called the Heralds, the Panthers, and the Wolverines. But when they moved in 1934, they came up with something new. After deciding to be the Lions—they wanted to stay consistent with the jungle-cat image of baseball's Detroit Tigers—two lion cubs were given to the team by John Millen of the Detroit Zoo. Their names were "Grid" and "Iron." And, unbelievably, the lion cubs accompanied the team to all of their games, undoubtedly adding a little more life to the sideline.

In their second season in the league, the Lions won their first championship when they defeated the New York Giants 26–7.

They moved to Briggs Stadium (later known as Tiger Stadium) in 1938 and defeated Pittsburgh 16–7 in the first game.

In 1940, Chicagoan Fred Mandel bought the club. Stars of that era included Hall of Famers Bill Dudley and Alex Wojciechowicz, plus John Greene, Byron "Whizzer" White, Frank Sinkwich, and "Camp" Wilson.

That group, led by Richards, owned the Lions until 1948 when they were purchased for $165,000 by a syndicate headed by Edwin J. Anderson. Bo McMillin was named general manager and head coach.

History has proven that George A. Richards knew what he was doing when he bought the franchise and moved it to Detroit.

41 RIP Chuck Hughes

In Lions' history, Chuck Hughes would be barely a blip. On the all-time roster, he fits between Vernon Huffman and Jim Hunnicutt.

A back-up wide receiver with an ever-ready smile, Hughes didn't see much action. A native Texan, Hughes proudly wore cowboy boots and a Stetson hat. His teammates called him "The Coyote." In five NFL seasons he caught just 15 passes. Hughes never scored a touchdown.

It wasn't for how he lived that we remember Hughes, however, it was for how he died. On October 24, 1971, with 62 seconds left in a Lions game against the Chicago Bears at Tiger Stadium, Hughes grabbed his chest and collapsed on the field while running back to the huddle after an incomplete pass intended for tight end Charlie Sanders.

Chuck Hughes never regained consciousness. He was dead at the age of 28.

At first no one seemed to notice him sprawled out around the 25-yard line in the left-field sector of the park. Chicago's Dick Butkus was the first to see him on the ground and waved for help.

Hughes didn't move, his legs were crossed. He was given mouth-to-mouth resuscitation by one team doctor while another pounded on his chest, valiantly trying to get a heartbeat.

Later, Dr. Richard Thompson told reporters that Hughes' heart stopped on the field, and the doctors thought they got it going one time but couldn't be sure and then it stopped again.

He was taken off the field on stretcher as the stunned crowd of more than 50,000 fans watched. By now they knew exactly what was going on after watching doctors trying to bring No. 85 back to life.

Hughes was treated by four cardiologists and other medical personnel at Henry Ford Hospital where he was declared dead at 4:41 PM. His wife, Sharon, collapsed at the hospital. They had a 23-month-old son.

Prior to running back to the huddle, Hughes had caught a 32-yard pass and received a severe jolt when he was crushed between two Chicago defenders—Bob Jeter and Garry Lyle. But Lions quarterback Greg Landry said Hughes appeared okay when he returned to the huddle. It was his first reception of the season.

An autopsy revealed that he had heart disease that had been coming on for years. There was no evidence to connect his death to the physical activity of the game.

The official cause of death was "arteriosclerotic coronary artery disease with acute coronary thrombotic occlusion."

A bony 180-pound and 6', no one would have thought Hughes would be a candidate for heart disease. After an injury in a pre-season game just six weeks prior, he was put through a battery of tests, including electrocardiograms and blood work. No sign of heart problems was found.

Afterward, owner William Clay Ford was shaken up like everyone else. "Never, never in the wildest moments would you ever believe a thing like this could happen. It's just inconceivable."

Hughes, one of 13 children, played college ball at Texas–El Paso. He was a good friend of PGA golfer Lee Trevino, and Hughes was well liked by his teammates.

That day he got into the game after Larry Walton, the Lions regular wide receiver, re-injured a leg muscle in the second half. Hughes caught his first and only pass of the season.

The Lions lost 28–23 that day, but the score didn't matter. They had lost one of their own, one who was way too young to die. He was buried in San Antonio, Texas, with all 40 of his teammates in attendance, along with Coach Joe Schmidt.

All these years later, Hughes remains the only NFL player who has lost his life on the field.

42 Tiger Stadium, A Longtime Home

Don't let those Tigers baseball fans hog all the warm and fuzzy memories of their once beloved but now demolished Tiger Stadium.

They get all sentimental, sometimes close to tears, thinking about the stadium that oozed character, featured the wondrous aroma of fresh-mown grass, and sold the tastiest red hots anywhere. Ernie Harwell had his perch in the radio booth. Oh, and their Tigers won World Series championships there in 1968 and 1984.

Denny McLain, Mickey Lolich, Al Kaline, Mark Fidrych, Alan Trammell, Sparky Anderson, need I go on?

That's all fine and good, but remember that Tiger Stadium was home to the Lions for 37 years, too. The Lions, who have never been to a Super Bowl, actually won two of their four championships at the corner of Michigan and Trumbull.

It was the perfect old stadium for baseball and football. Perfect, except for the times your dad came home with tickets to the game and then when you found your way to your seats there was a post between you and Willie Horton or Charlie Sanders or Mel Farr. The posts were easier to deal with when you were younger or on free bat day when the constant pounding of real full-size bats took your attention away from everything except the game. (Can you imagine if they did that today? Free full-sized bats? Not a chance.)

It was better when your dad brought home box-seat tickets. No posts, no impediments. It was a perfect spot to witness your first NFL game—it was so much better than on television—and fall in love with the game all over again.

The Lions won their 1935 championship at the University of Detroit Stadium. In 1938 they moved to Briggs Stadium, the former name for Tiger Stadium, which had a capacity of 53,000.

The football field was located mostly in the outfield, running from the right-field line to left-center field parallel with the third-base line. The benches for the Lions and their opponents were on the outfield side of the field. The Lions played there until 1974, but even after they left, a possession symbol and its light bulbs for football games could still be seen on the left-field auxiliary scoreboard.

Perhaps the Lions should have stayed at Tiger Stadium longer. After all, they played three playoff games at the old ball park and—are you ready for this—they won all three. Yes, I'm talking about your Detroit Lions.

In 1952, before a crowd of 47,645, they beat the Los Angeles Rams 31–21 and a week later went to Cleveland and beat the Browns for their second NFL championship. A year later they won back-to-back NFL championships by defeating the Cleveland Browns 17–16 at Briggs Stadium before 54,577 fans.

Then in 1957 the Lions won their fourth NFL championship with a 59–14 win over Cleveland (Browns fans must have hated the Lions), again at Briggs Stadium in front of 55,263 diehards.

In 1968, there was talk in Detroit that the Lions and Tigers were looking into building a new sports facility. Initially a dual stadium complex was discussed that included a moving roof, but it was dismissed because of high costs and lack of commitment from the Tigers. In 1973, ground was broken for what became the Pontiac Silverdome. The Lions played their final game at Tiger Stadium in 1974, their final outdoor home game.

The hale and hearty Lions fans, who had endured November and December snow and sleet storms to see their Lions, moved to a climate-controlled dome. It wasn't a sad move but more of a look to the future.

43 Add This to Your Bucket List

When Rob Sims was traded to Detroit from Seattle, he couldn't have been more pleased.

Playing with the Seahawks was fine if you're crazy about coffee, but Detroit is in the middle of football country. It's also part of the NFC North, often referred to as the Black and Blue Division.

Making a trek to all three divisional cities—Chicago, Green Bay, and Minneapolis—is a must for a Lions fan. If it's not on your bucket list, you ought to rethink your priorities.

Let's start with Chicago. Chicago's Soldier Field sits on the shores of Lake Michigan. In September and perhaps October, sailboats bob on the lake clearly visible from the historic field.

Like Lions' fans, Bears fans are passionate. So wear that Lions' jersey with pride but be ready to take some grief. Years ago a bunch of Michigan State students made the trip to cheer for the Lions and were told by a security guard if they didn't take off their Lions' jerseys he couldn't guarantee their safety.

It's a newer and kinder world out there these days. And a little grief is worth it for a weekend in Chicago, one of the best cities in the country with its shopping along the Miracle Mile of Michigan Avenue, great restaurants, and music. You can find a cheap flight, drive, or take the train. Just get there.

Green Bay is slightly different as far as cities go. It's small, but the folks are friendly. And no one goes to Green Bay for anything other than to experience Lambeau Field. Do they?

The trick to seeing the Lions at Lambeau is to find a ticket. Plan ahead, and call in all your connections. It's worth it to pull onto Lombardi Avenue and into the parking lot to breathe in the aroma of grilling bratwurst. There's nothing anywhere like it.

The Cheeseheads are a friendly people. A little smug about their team? Perhaps. But why wouldn't they be? Give yourself time to go through the Packers museum or put it on your agenda for the day before the game. You don't have to be a Packers' fan to appreciate it, just a fan of football.

Beware—hotel rates are jacked up on Packers weekends. But nearby Appleton (about a 25-mile drive) offers plenty of hotel space at normal rates. Direct flights from Detroit are available to Green Bay and Appleton. Or you can fly into Milwaukee and make the two-hour drive through Cheesehead country.

The Vikings fans have created an environment at the Metrodome where it's extremely loud and difficult for opponents. Then there's the annoying sound of the horn they blow whenever they score—or whenever they feel like it.

The Metrodome is near extinction, and it can't happen soon enough. Of all the NFL stadiums, it's the one that's closest to being a dump. Since the roof fell thanks to snow in 2010, the replacement roof creates a much brighter experience.

Perhaps the best thing about the Metrodome is that it's situated right downtown. There's light rail service that stops at the stadium, if you're staying out by the airport or the Mall of America.

Downtown Minneapolis features good restaurants, bars, and an old-fashioned Macy's that seems to cover a city block (it doesn't but it's huge). Hotels are abundant, and reasonable rates can be found. If you've never been to the Mall of America, it's worth a trip for the magnitude of it. Bring money. Minnesota is a great place to shop because there's no sales tax on clothing.

There you go, now get going.

44 No Happy Ending

It could have been a storybook tale. Steve Mariucci, native Michigander, returned home to coach the Detroit Lions. Mariucci was born in Iron Mountain, in Michigan's Upper Peninsula. He was quarterback at Division II Northern Michigan University. He is also best friends with Michigan State basketball coach Tom Izzo, another Iron Mountain native.

Lions fans had longed for a big-name coach whose resume had success written all over it. They needed a coach who could turn the ship around. Mariucci fit the bill, but there was no happy ending. Actually, it was quite disastrous.

The Lions were coming off a 3–13 season in 2002 and trying to wash away bad memories of Marty "I'll Take the Wind" Mornhinweg.

Lions general manager Matt Miller hired Steve Mariucci, who became the 22nd coach in franchise history. Mariucci was hampered by Millen's personnel decisions and draft picks. One problem was quarterback Joey Harrington, who had been drafted with the third overall pick in 2002 and never lived up to expectations. Mariucci, who earlier in his career had been the quarterbacks coach at Green Bay who helped Brett Favre, couldn't get the best out of Harrington.

In 2003, Mariucci's first season, the Lions started 1–6 and finished 5–11. In his second season, the Lions got off to a hot start, winning 4-of-6, but then they lost five straight and finished a disappointing 6–10.

Mariucci didn't make it all the way through season No. 3 in Detroit. The Monday after a 27–7 blowout loss to the Atlanta Falcons on Thanksgiving, Mariucci was fired. Millen had struggled with the decision over the long weekend. He said the NFL is a brutal business and sometimes good people suffer a cruel fate. In his two-plus seasons in Detroit, Mariucci had accumulated a 15–28 record.

After six seasons (1997–2002) as head coach of the San Francisco 49ers, Mariucci was reportedly let go because of a power struggle with the general manager. In Mariucci's final season with the 49ers, they finished with a 10–6 record and won their playoff wild-card game only to get blown out at the division level by Tampa Bay, the eventual Super Bowl champs.

Mariucci had accumulated a 60–43 record in San Francisco including playoffs and had taken he 49ers to the playoffs four of his six seasons.

Steve Mariucci was fired by the Lions on November 28, 2005. He has never coached again, but he maintains a high profile with work on the NFL Network.

45 Once a Fan, Now President

As Lions president, Tom Lewand has a different perspective than many NFL team executives. Lewand grew up in the Detroit area, and yes, he was a Lions fan surrounded by other Lions fans.

Lewand has spent 17 seasons working with the Lions in varying capacities. Early on he was the salary-cap guru and then had stadium development added to his duties when the Lions decided to move from the Silverdome and build a new stadium in downtown Detroit.

All along the way his perspective as a fan has been part of who he is and how he operates. Lewand said some of his most memorable moments with the Lions have involved the old-timers and many Hall of Famers who played for the Lions while Lewand was growing up.

"We had the 1957 [championship] team anniversary dinner, then we had the Paper Lion reunion that we did at Henry Ford, then we had the 75th anniversary team," Lewand said. "To be around guys like Joe Schmidt, Yale Lary, Dick LeBeau, Lem Barney, and Greg Landry. There's some great guys who have played the game and guys that I grew up watching and following that I had a tremendous respect for as a kid growing up.

"Those are special opportunities and lasting memories, and I will never be a person who loses sight of the value of the contributions those guys have made or how important they are to our history," Lewand added.

These days Lewand is in charge of the overall direction of the team. He has worked closely with Martin Mayhew as general manager and Jim Schwartz as coach to get the Lions turned around. The three of them started working together after the 0–16 season in 2008, and in 2011 they saw their hard work pay off with a 10–6 record and a trip to the playoffs.

Lewand negotiates player contracts and oversees all day-to-day business of the team and Ford Field. This includes management of finance, football administration, player development, security, equipment operations, medical, ticketing, sales and marketing, public/media relations, broadcasting, and human resources. He also oversees Ford Field operations and administration, acquisition of events, and the development of Ford's lease space. He was instrumental in overseeing Super Bowl XL that was held at Ford Field in 2006, the 2009 NCAA Final Four, and other major sporting and entertainment events.

Like all Lions' fans, he's passionate about the team and the city of Detroit.

He tells a story of bringing in Luis Perez as the team's new chief financial officer in the 2011 off-season. Perez had most recently worked with the Baltimore Ravens and prior to that with the Knicks and Rangers at Madison Square Garden.

First Lieutenant Reports

When the Lions drafted Caleb Campbell, they were assured that he would be able to sign right away even though they were getting him out of West Point. On the eve of his signing, the rules changed. Campbell had to stay in the Army for two more years. Patiently he waited. Well, he worked out—including a stint with the U.S. Bobsled team—while he waited for his shot in the NFL.

When he finally signed, the Lions brought out a box of his T-shirts and workout wear from two years previous. Turns out that they were now too tight. He'd grown stronger and bigger waiting for his chance. He grew so much that they moved him from safety to linebacker. First Lieutenant Campbell made the practice squad as a rookie and played in two games. His first was in his home state of Texas against the Dallas Cowboys. A soldier Campbell didn't know sent him a flag from Afghanistan to keep in his locker. Campbell was humbled and honored. The Lions cut him after the 2011 training camp.

"He came here, we were coming off last season (6–10), the four-game win streak at the end was great, but we weren't there yet. And he looked around and said, 'Boy, I saw a lot more Ravens stuff in Baltimore, I don't get the feeling around here.'

"I said, 'You don't understand, just wait when we get going. Just wait.'"

Perez noticed a lot of Tiger 'D' Baseball hats but he wasn't seeing Lions fans showing their colors.

"I said, 'I can tell you don't get it. I can't explain to you, I can't articulate just wait.' About half-way through the season, I think we were 5–0, maybe it was the Monday night game he said, 'I think I get it now.'"

Tom Lewand has gotten it all along because he was a fan first and a team president later.

46 Monte Clark's Two Stints

The Lions got rid of Monte Clark once. After seven seasons, capped off with a 4–11–1 disappointment, Clark was fired as the Lions head coach.

The Lions were coming off a 9–7 season and a playoff loss when Eddie Murray missed a 42-yard field goal in San Francisco. The Lions were preseason favorites to win the division, but they won just one of their first six games after Billy Sims was knocked out for the season with a knee injury.

But even at the end, even after the final game, Clark was resolute. He had three years remaining on his contract and was not going to resign.

He knew that he could be fired and said that nothing in the NFL surprised him. After all, they couldn't fire everybody.

So he was fired a few days after the miserable 1984 season. Clark had only finished with winning records in two of this seasons (1980, 1983). In Clark's second season, quarterback Gary Danielson was injured in the preseason and lost for the year. Many blamed the Lions' struggles on Lions general manager Russ Thomas, not Clark.

Still, William Clay Ford fired Clark, telling him it was a tough decision.

Clark, though, was not quite done with the Lions.

He took five years off after being fired by the Lions, then went to work for the Dolphins as director of player personnel and then offensive line coach for a year. In 1998 he was an assistant at the University of California–Berkely. He resigned after one year.

Then in 1999 he returned the Lions as a special advisor. He was always around during the Bobby Ross years and stayed on when

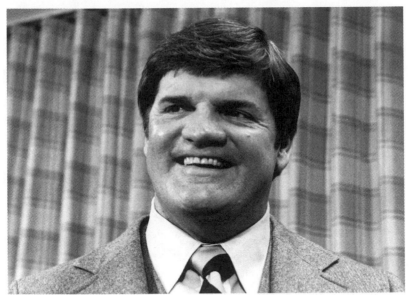

In this January 11, 1978, file photo, Monte Clark smiles as he was introduced during a news conference as the new head coach of the Detroit Lions football team in Pontiac, Michigan. Clark coached the Lions for seven years and led them to the playoffs in 1982 and 1983. (AP Photo/ Richard Scheinwald)

Matt Millen arrived. Clark, a former Cleveland Browns offensive tackle whose specialty was the offensive line, often would write up reports, particularly on the offensive linemen.

Clark also worked with the pro scouts. Occasionally during training camps he would work with the offensive line. Also, he'd be given special projects.

"Matt one time had him take a look at our whole roster 'give me another perspective on it let me see what somebody with a dispassionate perspective would have,'" Lions president Tom Lewand said.

"He was always welcome, he was here a lot. During Matt's time he traveled with us."

Clark was a character with an unmatched, dry sense of humor.

Ask him about his golf game, and he had one response: "Well, I just had my ball retriever re-gripped again. That's never a good sign."

Clark was also deeper than he might have appeared.

Early in the 1980 season, quarterback Gary Danielson and his wife lost a daughter, Kaity, who was 7 days old, due to a viral infection. In 1961 Clark and his wife had lost a 3-year-old daughter to leukemia. Clark had written a poem about her called, "Gone for a Time." He gave a copy of that poem to Danielson.

Clark died on September 16, 2009, at age 72 after bone cancer spread to his liver and lungs. That poem was printed on his memorial card, along with his personal philosophy:

"Watch your thoughts for they become your words...

Watch your words for they become your actions...

Watch your actions for they become your habits...

Watch your habits for they become your character...and

Watch your character for it becomes your destiny."

47 Don't Forget Mongo or Karras

Alex Karras didn't win an Oscar for his performance as Mongo in *Blazing Saddles* but it was an unforgettable performance. As a somewhat slow thug in a 10-gallon hat, Mongo rode into town on a brahman bull and knocked out a horse with one punch.

Before Karras was perfectly cast as Mongo, he was a defensive tackle for the Lions from 1958–1970. He had a one-year break—1963—while he served a suspension along with Green Bay Packers halfback Paul Hornung—for admitting they made bets on NFL games.

A stubborn fellow, Karras was told to stay away from the famous Detroit bar, the Lindell AC, by commissioner Pete Rozelle who claimed it was a gambling haven. In total defiance

Karras bought shares in the bar and became a bartender there during his suspension. Also during that time off, he returned to pro wrestling, which he first became interested in after college and before signing with the Lions as a first-round draft pick in 1958. This time around he took on Richard Afflis, better known as Dick the Bruiser. One night at the Lindell AC, the two were goofing around to promote their upcoming fight when a patron mistook it for a real fight and broke a cue stick over Dick the Bruiser's head. A brawl ensued that got national attention, pretty good promotion for the upcoming wrestling match that Karras unfortunately lost.

Karras got out of the bar business, much to Rozelle's delight, and was reinstated to the NFL in March 1964.

On the field, Karras was a force. From 1958 to 1970 the Lions were better than .500 in six of those 13 seasons. They only made the playoffs once, in 1970, despite an 11–3 record in 1962 and 9–4–1 in 1969.

In his only playoff game (1970), Karras and the Detroit defense didn't allow a touchdown but lost 5–0 to the Dallas Cowboys. It turned out to be the final game of Karras' career. He injured his knee late in the 1970 season and then reported to training camp in 1971 knowing his job was in question. After a less than stellar preseason, Karras was released, ending his career at the age of 35.

Karras always had a problem with his coaches.

He quit playing for the Iowa Hawkeyes more than once after disagreements with his coach Forest Evashevski. In his senior season, in 1957, Karras won the Outland Trophy as the most dominant lineman in the nation. He was also a runner-up in Heisman Trophy voting, which was and still is unusual for a lineman. In 1977 he was selected to the Iowa Sports Hall of Fame, and in 1991 he was inducted into the College Football Hall of Fame.

After he battled with Lions coach George Wilson, Karras asked for a trade. Instead, Wilson was fired in 1964. Karras didn't get along with his replacement, Harry Gilmer, either. Gilmer and Karras sparred, and eventually Gilmer was fired and replaced by Joe Schmidt, Karras' former teammate.

The football field wasn't big enough to contain Karras who found new careers in television and the movies.

He played himself in the 1968 film adaptation of George Plimpton's book, "Paper Lion."

Karras spent three seasons as an analyst on *Monday Night Football,* and he made guest appearances on television shows such as *M*A*S*H** and *The Odd Couple.* In the 1980s played the father, George Papadapolis, on the TV show *Webster* alongside his real-life wife Susan Clark.

48 The Calvin Rule

When Calvin Johnson went up for a game-winning 25-yard touchdown catch at Chicago's Soldier Field to open the 2010 season, he could have never imagined the uproar that would follow for days, weeks, and years to come.

Since then it's been called The Calvin Play. And if you follow the NFL, you know the story and the controversy.

But do you understand the rule? Welcome to the club.

Remember the play?

With 26 seconds left and the Bears up 19–14, Shaun Hill (who was in for an injured Matthew Stafford) found Johnson in the end zone. Johnson went up against the Bears' Zack Bowman and caught the ball. He got two feet down and then appeared to have control with one hand when he put the ball on the ground.

One official signaled touchdown. For a few seconds, the Lions thought they had pulled off a big win over the Chicago Bears. Then the ruling came down that it was an incomplete pass.

"I figured after I got two feet and a knee down, to me it was a catch. That's why I got up and took off. But it is what it is, you can't go back," Johnson said.

Here's the rule (NFL Rule 8, Section 1, Article 3, Item 1): "If a player goes to the ground in the act of catching a pass (with or without contact by an opponent), he must maintain control of the ball after he touches the ground, whether in the field of play or the end zone. If he loses control of the ball, and the ball touches the ground before he regains control, the pass is incomplete. If he regains control prior to the ball touching the ground, the pass is complete."

Lions coach Jim Schwartz said there was no doubt Johnson caught the ball.

"He made a great catch, went up, had a one-on-one, he jumped like we've seen him jump. He has possession of the ball, he has two feet down, he goes to the ground, lands with a butt, goes to turn over and puts the ball on the ground and loses it there," Schwartz said.

"In the league's eyes, the spirit of the rule is if you go to the ground in the process of a catch, you have to come up with a football, it makes it easy to officiate, it makes it black and white, I can respect that. I understand that," the coach added.

He was being a gentleman because the rule remains controversial. The NFL Competition Committee reviewed it but decided not to change it in March 2011.

It's written in black and white but not that easy to call. It's subjective and varies from official to official.

Credit Schwartz in the situation with not blaming the loss on the call.

Credit Calvin Johnson for handling the whole deal like a professional, as always.

But give the fans credit, too. They invest heavily in following the Lions—and I'm not necessarily talking about tickets and concessions. They want a fair playing field. With the rule as it stands, one official could call it a touchdown while another could say it is not.

The officials clearly cost the Lions a touchdown in their 2011 regular season finale at Green Bay. It wasn't the same rule, but Titus Young caught a touchdown pass in the end zone and the replay clearly showed he had both feet in and had control of the ball. It was ruled incomplete, and Schwartz had no challenges left due to two earlier questionable calls. Scoring plays are always reviewed, but this was not a scoring play so it wasn't automatically reviewed. It cost the Lions six points. Had it counted, it could have changed the entire complexion of the game, which was a close one.

After the Calvin non-catch, Lions veteran linebacker Julian Peterson said only half kiddingly that the Lions wouldn't start getting calls in their favor until they became winners. It's tough to win when you're fighting both the opponent and the rules.

49 Creekmur's Wait Pays Off

During high school and their early pro years, players were considered sissies if they wore facemasks. Lou Creekmur was no sissy. Because of this, his nose was broken and reset 13 times. He had that flat-nose look because most of the cartilage in his nose was gone.

Broken noses didn't keep him out of games, though. He was one durable warrior, but his dementia in the last 30 years of his life could be attributed to so many hits in the head.

He died at age 82 in July 2009 from complications of dementia following a 30-year decline that included cognitive and behavioral

Consistently Excellent

Who among the Lions has been selected the most times for the Pro Bowl?

The top two should not be a surprise, but No. 3 and No. 4 might be a little tougher.

Joe Schmidt and Barry Sanders are tied at the top with 10 selections each. Coming in at No. 3 is safety Yale Lary with nine and tackle Lou Creekmur with 8. All four have been selected to the Pro Football Hall of Fame.

issues such as memory loss, lack of attention and organization skills, and increasingly intensive angry and aggressive outbursts.

An autopsy showed he had developed chronic traumatic encephalopathy. He was the 10th former NFL player diagnosed with the disease.

It was a sad ending for Lou Creekmur who was inducted into the Pro Football Hall of Fame in 1996. He played 10 seasons for the Lions.

Offensive players from the 1950s such as Bobby Layne and Doak Walker, get much credit for the Lions' three championships (1952, '53 and '57). Just don't leave Creekmur out of the conversation. He mostly played on the offensive line at guard and tackle. In critical short-yardage situations, he also played on the defensive line. He spent 1955 filling in at defensive tackle following Les Bingaman's retirement.

Creekmur had apparently been left out of Hall of Fame conversations for years. He was eligible in 1964 but had to wait 32 years for the call.

"There is gold at the end of the rainbow, I can attest to that. Good things do happen to those who wait," Creekmur said in his acceptance speech.

He was presented by Doak Walker, his former teammate.

"I waited a long time for this," Creekmur said, "but I tell you, it has not lost any of its luster."

It was a long indirect road that brought Creekmur to Detroit.

He was born in 1927 (he weighed 14 pounds) and graduated from high school in New Jersey in 1943. He then fought in World War II. He was drafted in the 26th round out of William & Mary in 1948 by the Philadelphia Eagles. He opted to pursue a Master's degree instead of football. Two years later, after he completed his eligibility, he was placed in a frozen player pool by the NFL. The Lions took him with their second-round pick in a special 1950 draft of those pool players.

He finished his college career and started his NFL career with the Lions. Creekmur played in 168 straight games until his initial retirement in 1958. That didn't stick though. At a luncheon in Detroit in the fall of 1958, Coach George Wilson told Creekmur that the Lions still needed him. He had missed the first four games of the season and hadn't practiced since 1958, but he started every game for the rest of that season. Then he called it quits for good.

Quarterback Bobby Layne was one of Creekmur's favorites, perhaps it was because Layne took starting offensive linemen out to expensive steak dinners to thank them and encourage them to keep on keeping him upright.

"Lou Creekmur's outstanding contributions to pro football are well documented," said Steve Perry, the Pro Football Hall of Fame's President/Executive Director when Creekmur died.

"He was truly an exceptional offensive linemen who quietly and effectively went about his business of blocking for runners such as Hall of Famer Doak Walker and protecting his quarterback Bobby Layne.

"Also, the fact that Lou achieved such a high level of success while playing multiple positions speaks volumes about his athletic ability, and it is part of what makes his legacy as a football player so unique."

50 Best Free Agent Signing Ever?

Dick LeBeau has spent 50-plus seasons as an innovative defensive coach in the NFL, most recently with the Steelers where Troy Polamalu has said LeBeau is the heart of the defense.

He's considered the father of the zone blitz, which he created in the late 1980s while coaching the Cincinnati Bengals.

But those accomplishments did not get him into the Pro Football Hall of Fame.

Thirty-seven years after retiring as a defensive back for the Detroit Lions, he was elected into the Hall of Fame. For years it had been an injustice that he wasn't considered one of the best of all time. It just took a little longer than most anyone would have thought for him to get the honor. The day of his induction, the whole Steelers' team was in attendance, and he mentioned them often in his acceptance speech.

"I might be off a little on this, Ike (Taylor), but when I first came there, I don't think I started him in one game. Now he's started every game we've played for the last six years. Hasn't missed a game, hasn't missed a snap. That's a great record of durability and dependability. Six straight years. Ike, all you got to do is go eight more, man, and you can catch me with a smile," LeBeau said that day.

It was with the Lions where he got his start. Actually taking it back farther, he played for Woody Hayes on Ohio State's 1957 championship team.

LeBeau was originally drafted by the Cleveland Browns, but they cut him. (Exactly who made that decision?). So the Lions signed him as a free agent, and he played for 14 seasons.

LeBeau became the full-time starting right cornerback in 1961, playing opposite another Hall of Famer, Dick "Night Train" Lane until 1965. Then Lem Barney took over Lane's position. Over a five-year span, the tandem of LeBeau and Barney set an NFL standard with 65 interceptions.

LeBeau, widely considered one of Detroit's greatest defensive backs in history, pulled in 62 interceptions for 762 yards and three touchdowns from 1959–72. Those 62 interceptions were the most by a player in Lions' history and eighth all-time in the NFL.

He was also durable, playing in 171 consecutive games and 185 games total. He went to three Pro Bowls (1964–66).

Perhaps he learned a little something from his defensive coordinator from 1960–62, a coach by the name of Don Shula.

"Don Shula was one of my first defensive coordinators. I've been told a lot of times that Coach Shula takes credit for a lot of the good things that I did. In fact, almost all the good things that I did. I always tell Coach Shula when I see him, I said, 'Don, that's fair because me and my defensive teammates take all the credit for making you the coach you turned out to be later on,'" LeBeau recounted in his acceptance speech.

LeBeau went on to coach at Philadelphia, Green Bay, Cincinnati, Buffalo, and of course, Pittsburgh.

But he was inducted into the Hall of Fame as a player for the Lions.

"As far as my playing ability, I was known as the guy who was just going to come to work every day. I was going to play hard every day. Might not always play good every play, but I was going to play the next play as hard. I learned that from London, Ohio, a small town about two hours from where we're standing," LeBeau said. "Honesty and hard work, that's about all they value down there. It sure has stood me in good stead."

51 Another One Bites the Dust

It was all work and not many smiles in the Lions' locker room in 1980.

That all changed when Jimmy "Spiderman" Allen heard the song, "Another One Bites the Dust," by Queen while driving to the airport on the way to play a preseason game in Cincinnati.

The Steelers had "We Are Family," and once Allen adopted the tune, the Lions hand their own theme song, too.

In 1979 the Lions had finished 2–14. They were looking to turn the corner in 1980. Lions fans have heard this story again and again, but I digress.

Detroit won its last preseason games, which set a tone.

Then they opened the season with a 41–20 win over the Los Angeles Rams, who were coming off a Super Bowl appearance, at Anaheim Stadium.

It was all falling into place.

Allen thought the song was contagious. It gave the Lions a feeling of camaraderie—kind of like together we stand, divided we fall.

Allen had played at Pittsburgh where he was used to winning and used to a much looser atmosphere than when he moved to Detroit.

There was just something about the tune or the lyrics to "Another One Bites the Dust."

Pretty soon David Hill, Charlie Weaver, and James Hunter started singing it. Then rookie Billy Sims, Gary Danielson, and Ken Callicutt joined in.

Coach Monte Clark was all for it. In fact, he brought in a feather duster for Allen to use as a prop in a video.

It wouldn't have been fun if the Lions hadn't kept winning.

In Week 2, the Lions dusted off the Green Bay Packers 29–7 on the road. Even today that would be a mighty accomplishment. Another one bites the dust.

The Lions had bitten the dust so may times it was time for someone else to bite it—at least that's how Allen saw it.

In Week 3 they were favored to beat St. Louis, and they did with a 20–7 score, although the game was closer and tougher than the score indicated.

The Lions won their fourth straight to start the season with a 27–7 win over the Minnesota Vikings at the Silverdome. It was their best opening season since 1956.

It wasn't enough to sing with Queen, so Allen made a recording with James Hunter and David Hill providing backup vocals.

They changed the lyrics.

Are you ready? Hey, are you ready for this?
Are you sitting on the edge of your seat?
Come and watch the Detroit Lions, that nobody seems to beat.
And another one bites the dust.
And another one bites the dust.
And another one gone... and another one gone... another one
*   bites the dust.*
Offense, defense, special teams
If you tangle with the Lions you know what I mean
Hey, we're gonna get you ...

It was hokey, but it was just what the city of Detroit needed. Everyone was singing it and cheering for the 4–0 Lions. The town once again had pride in their Lions. Everyone knew Jimmy "Spiderman" Allen. He was much more than a strong safety, he was the one who brought the music back to the team.

Then reality hit.

The Lions lost in Week 5 at Atlanta 43–28.

After that loss, Monte Clark admitted he wouldn't mind hearing the song again.

The Lions didn't make it to the Super Bowl that season (they had put a line in the song that they were Super Bowl bound). After the 4–0 start, the Lions lost seven of the next 10 and finished the season 9–7, putting them out of the playoffs.

It was fun while it lasted. And even though the losses added up, the Lions had energized themselves and their fan base with a catchy tune.

52 Jim Schwartz to the Rescue

Coach Jim Schwartz has elevated the fist pump to an art form. After a big play, and always after a win, it has become Schwartz's signature move.

It just took Lions fans a few years to see it regularly, and for good reason

Schwartz took over a team that had set an NFL record by finishing a season 0–16. No other coach has ever had such a monumental task facing him.

Schwartz liked two things about the team and none had to do with on-the-field talent. He liked the fan base. He knew the long-suffering, yet passionate Lions fans had stuck with the team through the darkest times. He also like the commitment to win coming from the top of the organization.

Schwartz, who grew up in Baltimore, wasn't shy about wanting to make a huge impact. Upon arrival, with his wife and three young children in tow, he said eventually he wanted his kids to say they grew up in Detroit.

So far, so good.

When the Lions hired Schwartz, they were unlikely to get a big name coach and heck, they'd been through that with Steve Mariucci, and it didn't exactly work out too well.

Schwartz didn't have head coaching experience when he was hired, but he had worked himself up through the coaching ranks. And the word "work" is not used accidentally. He started his NFL career in the Cleveland Browns' player personnel department as a college and pro scout. He also assisted Coach Bill Belichick on defense with film breakdowns and scouting reports. In other words, he started at the bottom.

In Detroit, Schwartz worked with general manager Martin Mayhew and team president Tom Lewand. Their goal was to build a team for the long run. They weren't looking for shortcuts, they wanted to do it right from the get-go.

Like any good coach, winning is essential and Schwartz won only two games in his first season (2009). It was clear to see in his Monday postgame wrap-ups that losing was hard for him.

The next season his Lions got off to a 2–10 start. Even then he was staunch in his belief that the team was on the right path, especially because of quarterback Matthew Stafford. Even though the Lions had nothing but pride to play for, Schwartz never gave up and his message got across. They won their final four games and in doing so snapped their NFL-record road-losing streak. A 6–10 record was naturally disappointing, but Schwartz's ability to coach was unquestioned after they won those final four games.

The team was fired up for the 2011 season. They earned their first berth to the playoffs with a 10–6 finish. This is when the Schwartz fist pumping began to flourish.

Perhaps it's a release for him.

Schwartz is one intense coach, just watch him on the sideline during a game. Or watch him at training camp when something does not go the way he planned.

> ### Longest-Tenured Coach
> You may not know his name, but Don Clemons been a part of the Lions coaching staff longer than anyone else. Clemons, a defensive assistant, completed his 27th season with the Lions in 2011.
>
> Jim Schwartz is the ninth head coach who he has worked under. Others include Darryl Rogers, Wayne Fontes, Bobby Ross, Gary Moeller, Marty Mornhinweg, Steve Mariucci, Dick Jauron, and Rod Marinelli.
>
> He has coached every position on defense. He started with the Lions in 1985 as the strength and conditioning/defensive assistant.

Two of his best moves came before he coached a single snap. He hired two former NFL head coaches as coordinators—Gunther Cunningham on defense, Scott Linehan on offense.

The three work magic together. It's not all magic all the time, but they are on the same page and they are consistent. Guys like Stafford have a better chance to grow under these coaches because they maintain a consistency important to the development of a team.

In Schwartz's first training camp and season, he hardly went a day without mentioning Jeff Fisher, who he had worked under at the Tennessee Titans. That gradually disappeared as Schwartz grew more comfortable in his position.

After the Lions finished 0–16 and fired coach Rod Marinelli, the question in Detroit was who would want to coach these Lions?

Jim Schwartz seemed to be a perfect fit.

53 He Took the Wind

It was a late July afternoon during his first training camp as coach of the Detroit Lions that Marty Mornhinweg will be remembered for the most.

Well, there's also his 5–27 record over two seasons (2001–02). And, of course, there's the day he took the wind.

But first things first.

On July 30, 2001, at the football stadium at Saginaw Valley State University, Mornhinweg was not pleased with the effort of his team—at all.

He threw his sunglasses to the ground 35 minutes into practice, told the players they were loafing, and sent them to the locker room.

And then he stormed off the field and made his grand exit by hopping on his Harley-Davidson and zooming away. He left a confused team in the dust, not to mention 3,000 fans who were there to watch a full practice.

Think of Marty Mornhinweg and that's the picture—him on a motorcycle—that will pop up from the recesses of your mind.

Wide receiver Johnnie Morton said when he saw Mornhinweg's shades hit the ground, he figured someone had messed up. Then everyone left the field as they were ordered to, so it was too late to put the pieces back together that day.

Players waited in the locker room to see if Mornhinweg would return and re-start practice. But he did not.

Linebacker Allen Aldridge said at the time he would have liked to know exactly why Mornhinweg left so the situation could be corrected.

Safety Ron Rice said that Mornhinweg definitely got his message across. He wasn't happy with the attitude. And, by chance, that was the new team slogan—The New Attitude—under Mornhinweg and general manager Matt Millen.

Ahh, the wind. Mornhinweg taking the wind jokes still pop up now and then in the Motor City.

It happened in a 2002 game against the Chicago Bears that went into overtime. The Lions won the toss, but Mornhinweg felt having the wind in his favor was more important than getting the ball despite having kicker Jason Hanson who had kicked a then-NCAA record 62-yard field goal in college for Washington State University.

Well, the Bears didn't play into his plan, scoring a field goal on their opening overtime drive.

It was a decision that was never forgotten by Lions fans, and some refer to him as Marty Moron-weg.

Mornhinweg, who wasn't known for his communication skills, never got control of his team—hence they only enjoyed five wins in two seasons.

Of course it was also Millen's first season with the Lions and his first as a general manager in the NFL.

Mornhinweg had never been a head coach and hasn't been one since that debacle—the 5–27 record, not the motorcycle ride. He had spent the previous four seasons as offensive coordinator/quarterbacks coach with the San Francisco 49ers.

The 2001 season was the rookie year for left tackle Jeff Backus and center Dominic Raiola.

Under Mornhinweg, the Lions lost their first dozen games and finished the 2001 season 2–14 and fifth in the NFC Central.

Mornhinweg didn't change the team's attitude enough for the 2002 season, either. The Lions started that season 3–5 but finished with eight straight losses. Joey Harrington, a first-round pick that year, was the quarterback.

After getting axed by Millen, Mornhinweg went to Philadelphia where he became the Eagles offensive coordinator in 2006. He found success there. Coordinators have no part in making decisions involving overtime and wind.

In Detroit he was replaced by Steve Mariucci who had a better resume but didn't find much success with the Lions, either.

54 Reggie Rogers Kills Three

Reggie Rogers was perhaps the biggest draft bust in Lions' history. It's worse than that, though. He was also one of the biggest draft disappointments in the NFL.

After being an All-American in 1986 at Washington and playing on the Washington Huskies 1984 national championship team, Rogers' NFL career lasted just 15 games and it had nothing to do with on-field injuries.

Rogers, a defensive lineman, was selected seventh overall by the Lions in 1987 from the University of Washington.

He was selected ahead of eight future Pro Bowlers—linebacker Shane Conlan, defensive tackle Jerome Brown, Hall of Fame cornerback Rod Woodson, quarterback Chris Miller, wide receiver Haywood Jeffires, offensive tackle Harris Barton, offensive tackle Bruce Armstrong, and quarterback Jim Harbaugh. Those were just the first-round picks.

Suffering with emotional problems, Rogers was able to play just a half-dozen games in this rookie season in Detroit. He became a patient at an emotional counseling center. Rumors were it was for treatment for chemical and alcohol dependency.

Hopes were high for his second season, but he put an end to that hope after only playing five games.

Rogers, who was accused of running a red light, slammed his car into another vehicle in downtown Pontiac, on Wide Track Drive at University, killing three teenagers on October 20, 1988.

He had a blood alcohol content of .15; the legal limit was .10.

The accident, which happened within a mile of the Pontiac Silverdome, where the Lions played and practiced, was the end of the road for Rogers in Detroit.

The Lions waived him in July 1989 due to the fact he broke his neck in the accident. Of course he was also charged with felonies. He was convicted for vehicular homicide, and Oakland County Circuit Judge Gene Schnelz gave Rogers the maximum sentence of 16-to-24 months in prison per count, with the sentences to be served concurrently.

When he was released he had brief stints with the Buffalo Bills (1991) and Tampa Bay Bucs (1992).

Rogers had basically put an end to his NFL career the night he slipped behind the wheel and killed three teenagers.

Prison time and the loss of a promising NFL career was not enough to teach Rogers life lessons.

In 2008 he was involved in a hit-and-run accident in Tukwila, Washington, that resulted in his arrest and a driving under the influence charge. It was his fifth DUI arrest in the state of Washington, going back to his college days. In 2011 he plead guilty to his sixth drunk driving charge in that state.

His lawyer claimed that his years of football (remember, he played only 15 NFL games) had given him chronic traumatic ecephalopathy, a progressive, degenerative disease of the brain found in athletes and other, with a history of repetitive brain trauma.

Not many bought that argument.

As it turns out Rogers was one of the Lions' saddest draft stories. A life wasted. A man who killed three teenagers and didn't learn from it.

Football is the least of the story. Except NFL teams are built through the draft The Lions could have used that draft pick for one of several future Pro Bowlers.

Instead, it was a wasted pick.

55 Lem Barney

While Lem Barney's memories as a Lions' Hall of Fame corner-back could fill a book, perhaps his fondest memory came in his first start.

He remembers it like it was yesterday instead of 1967. The Lions were playing the Green Bay Packers, winner of the 1966 Super Bowl. Quarterback Bart Starr and Coach Vince Lombardi liked to test rookies, so they had the young Barney on their radar.

On a second-and-7, wide side to the field to the rookie from Jackson State University, Starr took a three-step drop and threw a quick out to All-Pro Boyd Dowler. The way Barney remembers it, Starr saw him closing in and Alex Karras and Roger Brown were putting pressure on him when he threw it low and away like a good fastball pitcher would do to a good fastball hitter.

Barney dove, stretched out, and intercepted the ball, did a shoulder roll, and then got up and ran about 24 yards to the end zone. He slammed the ball into the turf and watched as it rose skyward, put his hands on his hips and said, "Lord, this is going to be easy."

Well, not exactly that easy, as Barney was to discover in his 11 years of playing cornerback with the Lions.

But he was off to a good start. As a second-round pick from Jackson State, Barney stepped right in and was named the NFL's Defensive Rookie of the Year with 10 interceptions, three of them returned for touchdowns.

That was his first of 56 interceptions and also the first of seven touchdowns returned off interceptions. He scored four other touchdowns—two on punt returns, one on a kickoff return, and one on a field goal return.

Barney wore No. 20, which was later worn by running backs Billy Sims and Barry Sanders.

Barney was named to the Pro Bowl seven times and in 1999 was ranked No. 97 in *The Sporting News'* list of the 100 Greatest Football Players.

His defensive coach with the Lions was six-time Pro Bowl defensive back Jim David. The two were so close that David gave

Hall of Fame cornerback Lem Barney (20) of the Detroit Lions carries the football on a kickoff return during the Lions 34–17 victory over the Los Angeles Rams on December 17, 1972, at the Los Angeles Memorial Coliseum in Los Angeles, California. (AP Photo/NFL Photos)

the induction speech at Barney's Hall of Fame presentation. After David died, Barney, who was a minister, performed the matrimonial services for David's grandson Sean Thornton and Laura Butler in 2009 at the Grosse Pointe Ware Memorial.

David had only the best things to say about Barney in a *Detroit Free Press* interview: "If there was ever anybody better than Lem, I never saw or heard of him. Nobody before or since measured up to him.... He had speed and quickness and great acceleration. He had good hands, too, and a willingness to hit. And he was smart, really a smart player; he never beat us with a dumb play."

Barney also had a recording career of sorts. In 1970 he and his teammate, Mel Farr, befriended Motown recording artist Marvin Gaye when he unsuccessfully tried out for the Lions. As a thank you, Barney and Farr sang background vocals on Gaye's classic, "What's Going On." Barney even won a Gold Record for his vocal stylings.

Barney also appeared as himself in the movie, *Paper Lion*, which was based on the book of the same name by George Plimpton.

Barney was inducted into the Pro Football Hall of Fame in 1992, the fifth cornerback to receive such recognition.

Within the year he was arrested after a traffic accident in Detroit on charges of drunken driving and possession of cocaine and marijuana. He was eventually cleared of the charges, but it tarnished his reputation and cost him his job at Michigan Consolidated Gas. He went to work for Farr who owned a chain of car dealerships.

Barney, who is a lay minister at his church, is active in Detroit area charities.

He's easy to spot around town. He's the Hall of Famer wearing his trademark bowler hat.

56 One Fearsome Dude

The first time you see Kyle Vanden Bosch wearing his orange-red contact lenses, it's a jolt to the system.

Who is this guy?

The veteran defensive end is intimidating enough at 6'4" with a bald, shiny dome and a goatee. Throw in the red eyes, and you've created one fearsome dude.

Looks aren't deceiving, either. He's a monster on the field, flying in off the end to punish quarterbacks.

Much of the Lions' success on the 2011 defensive line can be traced back to the day in March 2010 that the Lions signed Vanden Bosch as a free agent.

At a minute after midnight, the bewitching hour of free agency, Lions coach Jim Schwartz knocked on the door of Vanden Bosch's home in Nashville. The coach was carrying gifts, including a 2005 bottle of Opus One cabernet and three stuffed Lions (one for each of Vanden Bosch's kids) and assorted Lions' T-shirts and other paraphernalia.

Schwartz convinced Vanden Bosch that he could be involved in something special in Detroit. That plus a four-year $26 million contract lured him north.

As the Titans' defensive coordinator, Schwartz knew Vanden Bosch well. While the Lions were building from the ground up, they needed some veteran leadership and no one could better fill that role on defense than Vanden Bosch. This is a man who doesn't like to get beat in practice. Even veteran beat writers were amazed when they first saw Vanden Bosch at practice. He'd chase a play 30 yards down field. No one else did that. Who is this man?

Vanden Bosch's work ethic has rubbed off on his teammates.

After Ndamukong Suh was drafted and getting ready for his first off-season workout, Vanden Bosch sent Suh a text to be in the locker room at 6:00 AM. Rookies don't mess with Vanden Bosch, no one does. Vanden Bosch's career got off to a slow start, which isn't unusual for defensive linemen. Now he makes those around him better.

He was elected team captain by his teammates for his first two seasons.

Vanden Bosch missed the final five games of the 2010 season after injuring his neck. He underwent surgery to fuse two vertebrae in his spinal column. Months later he said his recovery was "a piece of cake" and that he had no lasting effects.

Vanden Bosch is not one to take time off from practice, but in 2011 the coaches convinced him to take Wednesdays off. He was still on the field—he just wasn't going through the drills. It saved his veteran body a bit, and he admitted late in the season he felt fresh in part due to his rest days. He doubled his sack number from the 2010 season, finishing 2011 with eight. He started the 2011 season with a sack in each of the first three games.

The line has taken on his personality, which can best be described as nasty. Vanden Bosch is good with that; he's been called worse.

"This defense is built to be fast and aggressive. This front, that's what we do. We're physical, the type of defense takes the fight to people and make things happen. The personality of this team is not to back down and to go after teams. That's what we're getting paid to do," Vanden Bosch said.

Defensive coordinator Gunther Cunningham said the Lions could not have turned the corner on defense without Vanden Bosch. He's that important.

He's had help from veteran defensive tackle Corey Williams. Between them they helped get the best out of younger guys.

Pain Train Silenced

Zack Follett just might be one of the few seventh-round picks to endear himself to Lions fans. Follett's hard work earned him a spot on the practice squad in 2009.

His hard work caught the coaching staff's eye, and Follett was brought up to the 53-man roster and put on all special teams units where he was a stand-out for his hard-hitting style. He earned the nickname the Pain Train—he even had T-shirts designed. He was so much of a standout that it was tough to keep him off the field. Follett was a starter at outside linebacker at the beginning of his second season.

He was big on social media—Twitter and Facebook—before many of his teammates had discontinued this new way to reach out to fans. After his rookie season, Follett posted a video on his Facebook page of him facing a Lion, an actual Lion. It was an older animal, but it still had teeth, and a mane and it growled.

Follett was unfortunately on the receiving end of a helmet-to-helmet hit at the Meadowlands on October 17, 2010, in a game against the New York Giants. He was carted off the field on a backboard. Later that night, he sent out a tweet that he was going to be fine. However, he never played another NFL game. He showed up at Lions' training camp the next August, but was cut.

Defensive end Cliff Avril had a career year in 2011 with 11 sacks. Second-year defensive end Willie Young made a huge step from his rookie season. Suh got support from Vanden Bosch after his two-game suspension for stomping on Green Bay's Evan Dietrich-Smith.

Vanden Bosch is a fearsome defensive end, but it's his off-field approach to the game that made him such an integral part of the Lions improved defense.

57 Detroit Lions Academy

It's one thing to write a check. It's another to take a role in the lives of middle school students.

The Lions have done that since the Detroit Lions Academy opened in 2001. The Lions, through their charities, donate $50,000 a year to the academy through Community Schools of Detroit. That's just to keep the school operational.

Situated in a residential neighborhood, it's an alternative middle schools that's part of the Detroit Public Schools, not a charter school.

It's a place for middle school students who aren't ready for the jump to high school.

"We need a smaller environment to work with the kids. We have seven teachers," principal Cheryl White said. "You have to be flexible and have a lot of patience because a lot of these kids are experiencing things that a lot of us won't experience in a lifetime."

Some have anger issues, and there's an occasional pregnancy even though students are in grades six through eight.

"They're older because of attendance, previous behavior issues, grade retention that may have occurred in the third or second grade when they didn't get the academic support that they need," White said. "Sometimes we have kids who are adjudicated or in foster homes or girls homes. They're in girls homes not because they did anything, but because a parent may have given them up."

It's also a school where the principal, teachers, and students can often be seen wearing Lions apparel.

The uniform is dark pants and white shirts, but the only exception is the Lions' gear that is given to the students and staff each year at Christmas.

"Sometimes they don't win and we still wear it," White says with a smile.

The school is supported by the Lions, but other support from the community is always welcome. The building is old, but the floors are well polished.

Like all Detroit schools, the budget is slim for the Academy and the needs are many.

That's where the Lions step in.

"During Christmas, the Lions organization adopt families [through the school]. A lot of people adopt kids, [but] they adopt families. They're very, very generous to kids.... Hopefully it will become contagious. They might not see it now, but when they get older they'll give back," White said.

Lions wide receiver Calvin Johnson has given tickets to Lions' game to students who achieve enough to deserve the honor.

The Lions have sponsored trips to Buddy's Pizza for honor roll students.

And throughout the year, Lions players will visit and talk to the children.

In recent years Lions' wives have pulled together and visited the school twice a month for workshops with girls who are specifically chosen. Most are 14 and 15 years old.

Stanton Gives and Gives

Drew Stanton, a Lions backup quarterback for five seasons, outdoes himself each year with his community involvement. In fact, for three straight years was recognized as the Lions' Robert Porcher Man of the Year for his efforts.

Stanton is a local who played at Farmington Harrison and then went on to Michigan State.

He established his own foundation in 2008 with the main goal to support programs at Special Olympics and the Children's Miracle Network. He started working with Special Olympics while at Michigan State.

Sessions have included nutrition lessons, crafts, a defense class, and more.

"They open their eyes to new hobbies. Last year they did yoga, and the girls were really into it. They provided the mats, the T-shirts, the gym shoes, they went the whole nine yards," White said. "They also bought T-shirts for the rest of the school. It's always the giving-back part."

The girls have made affirmation boxes where they list their goals and place them inside and dream pillows where they inserted their dreams.

"Character education, that's another part that the Lions wives help build in the girls. Just the fact they never miss an appointment. They don't disappoint these kids, if they say they are coming, they are here," White said. "They never disappoint these kids, and that's so critical because a lot of students have felt serious disappointment."

It's a learning situation that seems to reach in both directions.

"It makes you feel good, but it also makes you feel like maybe somebody's listening. It also makes me appreciate the life that my kids have," said Suzanne Lewand, wife of team president Tom Lewand.

58 Football Times Two

When it's fall in Michigan, there's nothing better than a football weekend.

It's easy to experience the best in college football and one of the best fan experiences in the NFL all in two days.

Start with a home game at Michigan Stadium where you'll be among 109,900 of your closest friends. Then take I-94 east to Detroit and take in a Lions game at Ford Field.

For the Michigan game, go in October or November to make sure you see a Big Ten match-up. The cupcake schools on the home schedule early in the season provide great competition—and once in a while they pull a shocker like Appalachian State did in 2007—but a Big Ten match-up will give you a good football game.

If you've never been to a game to watch the Michigan Wolverines, you must put it on your bucket list. It doesn't matter who you are cheering for (although it helps if you love the maize and blue), when you see the marching band take the field and hear them play the fight song, you'll be enjoying the best in college football.

It's outdoor football at its best. And a few more luxuries—more concessions stands, more rest rooms—were added with the recent renovation.

Get there early, parking is available but it fills up early with tailgaters. Ann Arbor Pioneer High School a few blocks away offers parking for a price. There's also parking on the university golf course.

If you're not tailgating, walk downtown for breakfast or lunch or just to check out the campus and get the flavor of the college town. It gets a little crazy around some of the fraternity houses, but remember it's college.

Zingerman's Deli is a classic go-to destination, but there are plenty of other good choices. One of this writer's favorite Ann Arbor spots—Washtenaw County Dairy—is just a block off the main drag and serves up incredibly large portions of quality ice cream at prices that won't break you.

Enjoy the game, and hit downtown afterward. Then get a good night's rest to prepare for attending a Lions' game on Sunday.

After a day of fresh air, you'll be headed inside at Ford Field, which is 10 years old but has aged gracefully.

If you want to tailgate in Detroit, the best option is several blocks away at the Eastern Market where they provide plenty of parking just for tailgaters along with a shuttle to Ford Field. Immediately around Ford Field, parking is available in lots and garages but they don't allow tail-gating.

If you'd prefer to have someone else do the cooking and provide the beverages, there are a few local places within walking distance where you'll find other fans tuning up for the big game. One is the Elwood Bar just across the street from Ford Field.

The Lions experience on the streets outside surrounding the stadium include inflatables and entertainment.

Once inside there are plenty of concession opportunities.

And, of course, there's now a talented team worth cheering for. Afterward, don't be in a hurry, check out Greektown or one of the casinos. Perhaps you'll be in a celebratory mood.

Now, none of this comes cheap. But instead of taking a weekend up north, a feast of football would be a great way to celebrate a fall weekend in Michigan.

59 Tailgate Haven

Unlike tail-gating havens such as Lambeau Field or Arrowhead Stadium, Lions fans can't pull up close to Ford Field, fire up the grill, and pop open a few beverages. Lions' tailgaters have their own version of heaven at the Eastern Market about six or seven blocks away. It's a good brisk 10–15 minute walk. But if that doesn't sound good, a shuttle is provided for service each way for a mere $5.

Eastern Market is such a Detroit classic that it's a good match for Lions fans who want more than to park and walk into the nearest entrance at Ford Field.

If you're thinking brats on the grill, well there is that. But this is one big party. It's not uncommon for dancing to break out in one of the covered sheds.

Prior to the October 10 Monday night game in 2011, it was a typical scene with a live band (on that date it was Banned from E.A.R.T.H., a Black Sabbath tribute band) and a bubbling hot tub that's been wired to work even in a parking lot far from home.

Fans are loud and proud with most of them wearing some type of Lions gear—jerseys, hats, whatever they have that is Honolulu blue and silver.

With several parking lots, Eastern Market can accommodate about 750 cars. And an estimated 3,000 tailgaters each game find that Eastern Market is the place to be.

Of course there might be offerings fans aren't expecting, too.

In 2011, an undercover reporter for a Detroit TV station broke the booty-lounge-gate story. They found an unlicensed mobile strip club operating at the Eastern Market as "The Booty Lounge" on game days. It was a windowless bus with stripper poles and various gentleman's clubs accouterments.

Tickets for the Eastern Market are $35 for cars/trucks, $70 for school buses, $125 for RVs, and $155 for motor coaches and hot tubs tailgate parking. Parking is only $10. Several of the restaurants, such as Vivio's Food & Spirits and Roma Cafe, provide free shuttle service with purchases at their restaurants.

It's a great situation for tailgaters because it includes the essentials like three large public restrooms, trash bags and bins for garbage, and coal bins to dispose of hot coals from the grill.

If you've never been to the Eastern Market, exactly what are you waiting for?

On Saturdays, especially spring through fall, it's estimated that 40,000 people flock to the Saturday market. The area features 250 independent vendors and merchants processing, wholesaling, and retailing food.

At the heart of the market is a six-block public market (site of tailgating) featuring open-air stalls with fresh fruits, vegetables, fresh-cut flowers, homemade jams, pasture and or grass-fed meat, and locally produced specialty products. Occasionally you might even see a goose or rabbit.

Many people get there early on Saturdays and have breakfast before, after, or while shopping. The Russell Street Deli serves up a good breakfast or lunch, as does Louie's Ham and Corned Beef, but there are plenty of other offerings, too.

Shops can be found that specialize in cheese, wine, poultry, meat, seafood, nuts, and more.

The Eastern Market is north of Gratiot on Russell Street. Or take I-75 to the Mack exit. Check out the Eastern Market website for maps for tailgating parking lots.

60 Third Title in Six Years

Usually NFL opponents prefer to downplay anything resembling a revenge factor. It wasn't that way with the 1957 Detroit Lions. Oh boy, they had something to prove and in a big way.

In the 1954 NFL Championship Game they had been humiliated 56–10 by the Browns at Cleveland. Three years later it was still eating at their guts.

So when the Lions had a chance for a rematch in the 1957 NFL Championship, nothing was held back. It was held on December

Blacked Out in Detroit

It's difficult to imagine, but the 1957 NFL Championship Game was blacked out on television within a 75-mile radius. NFL commissioner Bert Bell wouldn't lift the blackout—even though the game was sold out—because he said fans who had bought tickets had done so with the idea it would be blacked out.

Well, as someone once said, there's no one as ingenious as an indignant Detroiter.

Fans figured out that with huge antennas, they could capture the signal from the Lansing television station. At a Wyandotte gas station, 200 fans sat in the garage on chairs borrowed from a funeral director. The owner went erected a 55' antenna at a cost of $200. He even quit pumping gas to watch the game.

He wasn't the only one building an antenna for the game. There was more pattering on Detroit rooftops that day than there was on Christmas Eve.

After the Lions won 59–14, *Detroit Times* columnist Joe Falls had the perfect topper for his column: "They Blacked Out the Wrong City."

29, 1957, at Briggs Stadium, later known as Tiger Stadium, before 55,263 diehard fans.

The Lions were without quarterback Bobby Layne who had broken his leg in a game three weeks previous. Actually he was there but standing on the sideline, wearing an overcoat and a fedora, and leaning on crutches.

Quarterback Tobin Rote took control and threw touchdown passes of 78, 32, 26, and 24 yards. Not bad for a backup, eh?

When it was over, the Lions knew the sweet taste of revenge, beating the Browns 59–14. Cleveland had been a one-point favorite. Perhaps that provided a little more motivation.

It was the biggest scoring differential in the NFL Championship game since the 1940 Chicago Bears shellacked Washington 73–0.

It was the third championship title for the Lions in six years but the first since 1953.

While the offense was spectacular, the defense had five interceptions—one each by Joe Schmidt, Jim David, Gerry Perry, Terry Barr, and Bob Long.

The Lions got off to a strong start on both sides of the ball, which was key to the pummeling. Long intercepted Browns' quarterback Tommy O'Connell early in the first quarter and gave the Lions the ball on the Browns' 19-yard line, which set up a touchdown and a 10–0 lead.

Then Barr recovered a fumble by Cleveland's Milt Campbell on the ensuing kickoff, giving the Lions the ball on the Browns' 15 and expanding the lead to 17–0.

With a 17–7 lead early in the second quarter, the Lions faced a fourth down. Rote rejected a play sent in by Coach George Wilson who called for a field goal. Instead Rote set up in a field goal formation but at the last minute lifted the ball, ran to his right, and hit rookie end Steve Junker alone on the 6-yard line. Junker hauled in the ball and scored untouched.

"That was the play that kept us going," Wilson admitted later, even though it wasn't his call.

In six previous games against the Browns (five of them wins), the most Detroit could score was 20 points. On that day they topped that in the first 22 minutes.

O'Connell, the leading passer in the NFL, said afterward he had suffered a fractured left leg almost a month before and no one knew. He didn't use it as an excuse, though. As he told reporters, "My leg didn't bother me very much today."

It was a sweet ending to a Lions' season that got off to a bit of a rocky start when Coach Raymond "Buddy" Parker walked off the job four months earlier and called the Lions players "uncoachable." His assistant, George Wilson, was promoted to head coach and led the Lions to this championship, which paid each winning player $4,295.41.

After the game, Joe Schmidt, the team captain, was mobbed by fans who ran onto the field. He had gone back out to get his hands on the game-winning football. He couldn't get through the jam at the mouth of the tunnel. He somehow reached the clubhouse through the box seats. He said that trek was tougher than the game, but it was worth the effort.

"We did a lot of thinking about that 56–10 game in Cleveland. Now maybe they can do some thinking," Lions defensive back Jim David said.

61 Life Before Hanson

While it may seem that Jason Hanson has been the Lions kicker forever, Eddie Murray held the job for a dozen years prior to Hanson's arrival.

Murray thought he still had it and planned to compete to play in 1992. But just before a six-day minicamp in April 1992, he was told that after a dozen years his services were no longer needed.

Even though he was not too happy about how he had been let go, years later he came to the aid of Hanson prior to the Lions playoff game in Philadelphia in 1995. Since Steady Eddie Murray had kicked at Philadelphia's Veteran Stadium, he knew about the drafts and tunnels. So he showed up at the Silverdome before practice the week before the game. Veterans Stadium was a tricky place for kickers with the wind coming out of the maintenance area, from under the lower-level stands, and out of the tunnels.

At the time coach Wayne Fontes said it showed a touch of class on Murray's part. Perhaps he was impressed that Murray was helping the guy the Lions drafted to replace him. Perhaps Murray

Eddie Murray (3) lines up a field goal during a game against the San Francisco 49ers on Sunday, October 2, 1988, in San Francisco. (AP Photo/Greg Trott)

wanted to see the Eagles suffer a bit since they had cut him after he expected to be there for more of a long haul.

Murray would play for a half-dozen other teams—Kansas City Chiefs, Tampa Bay Buccaneers, Dallas Cowboys, Philadelphia Eagles, Minnesota Vikings, and Washington Redskins—after leaving Detroit in the spring of 1992.

His last full season was 1997 when he kicked in a dozen games for the Vikings.

In 1994, in his first of two stints with the Dallas Cowboys, he kicked three field goals in Super Bowl XXVIII to help the Cowboys win, earning his first and only Super Bowl ring.

In 1999 he kicked in four games for Dallas (7-of-9). And in 2000 for four games with the Redskins, he was 8-of-12.

Murray was drafted in the seventh round out of Tulane by Detroit in 1980. His rookie season resulted in his first trip to the Pro Bowl where he was named MVP. He was also elected to the Pro Bowl in 1989. And four times in his career he was named to the All-Pro team. He was also named to the NFL's 1980s All-Decade team.

For his career he was good on 352-of-466 attempts for 75.5 percent.

He remains the 15th highest scorer in NFL history.

Perhaps Murray is best remembered for the field goal he missed in the NFC Divisional playoff game at San Francisco. With the Lions trailing 24–23 with 11 seconds remaining, he narrowly missed a 43-yard attempt. Earlier in the game he had made a 54-yarder, which matched his career high. (The Lions wouldn't get back to the playoffs until 1991.)

Even though he moved around, Murray retained his home in suburban Detroit. And all has been forgotten, with Murray often participating in the Lions' charitable events.

62 Loud and Proud

Certain stadiums around the NFL have reputations for being extremely tough on opponents due to the noise factor.

One of them is the Metrodome at Minneapolis, where the Vikings fans are loud from start to finish. They add an annoying Viking horn that is blown whenever they score. The Lions won there in 2011 for the first time 1993.

Another is the Superdome, home of the New Orleans Saints. Of course, in recent years the Saints fans have had plenty to cheer about.

Ford Field has never been considered an especially unwelcome stadium for opposing teams. That started to change in 2011, and it was no coincidence that was also when the Lions started to win.

It all became very apparent on October 10, 2011, when the undefeated Lions hosted the Chicago Bears on *Monday Night Football*. The building was electric that night when the 4–0 Lions took the field in front of a national television audience.

Thanks to the screaming fans, the Bears were called for nine false starts—eight on offense, one on special teams. Obviously it was tough for the Bears' offense to get anything going in those conditions. The Lions won 24–13 to bump up record to 5–0.

Afterward Coach Jim Schwartz gave one of the game balls to the fans. The next home game a football was printed with the stats that mattered and displayed in the Ford Field concourse so the fans could have their photo taken with their game ball.

While the Lions never had another game that season where the opponent had nine false starts, there were so many that they started a tote board on the big screen that kept track of false starts in each game and the total for the season.

Roary Sees Action

Chiefs running back Jamaal Charles might not be a huge fan of Roary, the Lions mascot, and for good reason.

In the Lions' 2011 home opener, Charles tried to stretch for a first down along the sideline. His legs slid into the mascot and knocked him down. Roary was fine, never missing a snap. But Charles was out for the season with a torn ACL.

When Roary isn't working the sideline at Lions games at Ford Field, he's the spokesman for the Detroit Lions Kids Club and speaks at elementary schools across Michigan. He's also available for appearances.

The next home game, a loss to San Francisco, the 49ers were whistled for five false starts. The Atlanta Falcons tried to prepare for the noise by blasting the sounds of jet engines during practice. Perhaps that was the ticket, since they were only called for three false starts.

Schwartz and the players implored the fans to keep it up. After all, every team needs its fans to succeed.

The Lions fans had been faithful through the bad years, selling out most games. But there were games when the noise level was more library-like than of the NFL stadium variety.

Perhaps those were the years the fans got a little turned around in their thinking. Schwartz has always been nice when he mentioned it, but the Lions fans in his first two seasons had a habit of doing the wave even when the Lions had the ball. They were just excited. Most of them know football, but at times it would slip their minds that they should be quiet when the Lions have the ball. It's just an odd little thing.

If they can be loud enough to cause nine false starts in one game, perhaps they can try to top that record.

When the crowd is loud, the players are more revved up. They can hear it even if they don't acknowledge it. Ndamukong Suh said he can definitely hear when the fans are chanting "Suh, Suh, Suh."

It was a first step in 2011 to become one of the NFL's loudest venues. It's up to the fans to keep it up.

63 A Pair of Heisman Quarterbacks

After Greg Landry left Detroit after 1978, the Lions were always searching for the next franchise quarterback. Really the search lasted until they drafted Matthew Stafford in 2009.

After they failed by drafting one Heisman Trophy–nominated quarterback in 1986, four years later they drafted a Heisman Trophy–winning quarterback.

The Lions just didn't learn their lesson.

In 1986 Chuck Long, who was coming off his record-setting senior season at Iowa, was drafted by the Lions in the first round, 12th overall.

Hayden Fry, his Iowa coach, had once said that Long was "destined for greatness." But it didn't happen with the Lions or any NFL team.

Michigan State fans remembered Long very well. In his senior season, Long faked a handoff and ran in for a game-winning touchdown at East Lansing. It was a career game for Long who was 30-of-39 for 380 yards, and five touchdowns (four of them passing).

So it was understandable that hopes were high for Long, the 1985 Heisman runner-up.

As a rookie he got in his first game when starting quarterback Joe Ferguson was injured. Long's first pass attempt was complete for 64 yards against Tampa Bay. Good start.

He had his best season with the Lions in 1987 when he threw for 2,598 yards, 11 touchdowns, and 20 interceptions. Not exactly a good ratio. He was traded to the Los Angeles Rams in 1990. After a year in Los Angeles he returned to Detroit for the 1991 season but didn't attempt any passes.

With Long not delivering like they had hoped, the Lions were back in the quarterback market. So in 1990 with the seventh overall pick in the first round, they drafted Andre Ware, the 1989 Heisman Trophy winner who broke 26 NCAA records in three years at the University of Houston. He threw for 8,202 yards with 75 touchdowns and left for the draft after his junior year.

When Ware came to Detroit, he joined another Heisman winner in Barry Sanders who had won the trophy in 1988.

But Ware was just another guy on the Lions' quarterback carousel—another quarterback who raised hopes high but they disappointed fans once he arrived.

Wayne Fontes was the coach, and he preferred to start Rodney Peete who was often injured. When Peete was out, Fontes' first choice as a replacement was Erik Kramer.

Jolly Old England

While more and more NFL teams are playing overseas, the Lions played in their first and only game in England on August 9, 1993, in an exhibition against the Dallas Cowboys.

The drew 43,552 to Wembley Stadium in the American Bowl exhibition game, which ended in a 13–13 tie. The year before, 61,000 had witnessed the American Bowl. Super Bowl MVP Troy Aikman was recovering from back surgery, so he didn't play.

Andre Ware got the surprise start for the Lions but was replaced in the second quarter by Rodney Peete. Neither quarterback could get much offense going.

Dallas had a scare when Kenneth Gant was injured trying to tackle Barry Sanders. He was hauled off the field on a stretcher.

The Cowboys could have won it, but Lin Elliott missed field goals of 38, 54, and 44 yards in overtime.

The Lions finished the 1993 season with a 10–6 record.

Fontes would only play Ware when the Lions were out of playoff contention or they were so far down in a game they had no chance of a comeback.

Ware's best stretch came late in 1992 when he won two of three games.

He began the 1994 season with the Los Angeles Raiders but was released after several games. In 1995, he was signed by the expansion Jacksonville Jaguars but was cut before the season started. That was the end of his NFL career, although he did find some success in the Canadian Football League.

Heisman Trophy winners can't always transfer their college magic to the NFL. It happened 20 years ago and still happens today (see Tim Tebow).

Since Long and Ware were drafted, the whole process has changed. There should be much less chance of missing on such a high pick these days.

64 Landry a Standout

How bad has the Lions' quarterback situation been over the years? Greg Landry still holds the distinction of being the only Detroit quarterback elected to the Pro Bowl since the 1970 merger. That was a while ago—1971 to be exact. Landry was also voted to the All-Pro team that season.

Landry didn't put up gaudy numbers in his 11 seasons with the Lions, but he was good enough to stand out among other NFL quarterbacks.

In those 11 seasons he led the Lions to just one playoff appearance.

Landry, who played at the University of Massachusetts, was drafted in the first round in 1968 with the 11th pick overall. He was the first quarterback taken.

When Matthew Stafford started as a rookie, it was the first time a rookie quarterback had started for the Lions since Landry in 1968. Landry didn't make it through the whole season. In that opening game he was 15-of-31 for 231 yards, two touchdowns, and four interceptions in a 59–13 loss to the Cowboys at Dallas. Bill Munson took over for that season. In the 1969 season, Landry threw four touchdowns and 10 interceptions.

What made Landry stand apart was his running ability. He was a big guy at 6'4". While at Massachusetts he ran, and that didn't change when he got to Detroit, even though it took Coach Joe Schmidt a while to adjust. At first Schmidt told Landry to stay in the pocket, but he would run at least a few plays every game and it worked. So Schmidt caved in and told Landry to run whenever he wanted.

In fact a 1971 article in *Sports Illustrated* said that Landry was ahead of his time. "It is this remarkable blend of hand and foot that makes Landry something special, the harbinger of things to come in pro football, the doomsayer of the last days of the dropback passer."

In 1970 Landry helped lead the Lions to a 10–4 record and their first playoff appearance in 13 years—they lost 5–0 at Dallas.

When he threw for 2,237 yards and 16 touchdowns in 1971, it was more than just a Pro Bowl season—it was also his best year as a Lion based on yardage. The only season he passed for more yardage was in 1979, his first season in Baltimore, when he passed for 2,932 yards, 15 touchdowns, and 15 interceptions.

In his 84 starts over 11 seasons in Detroit the Lions went 40–41–3. Landry remains third on Detroit's all-time career yardage list with 12,451 yards and second in touchdown passes with 80. Twenty of those touchdown passes were caught by Hall of Fame tight end Charlie Sanders.

Two Good Seasons

Lions quarterback Jon Kitna started every game in 2006 (3–13) and 2007 (7–9) and threw for 4,000 yards in each season, a franchise record that still stands.

In 2008, he was injured and placed on injured reserve in Week 5. Kitna said the injury wasn't that serious, and he could have returned that season. But when the Lions couldn't find any team that wanted to trade for a backup, they placed him on injured reserve.

The Lions had no replacements up to the task and finished the season 0–16. In the spring of 2009, the Lions drafted quarterback Matthew Stafford with the first overall pick.

Landry left for Baltimore after the 1978 season and played three seasons there.

After changing into coaching mode, he made a return to the Lions in 1995 as the quarterbacks coach under Bobby Ross. Landry tutored quarterback Scott Mitchell to a record-setting season in 1995 when the Lions were the top offensive unit in the NFL.

Landry's NFL career had come full circle. He was drafted by the Lions, played 11 seasons, then moved on elsewhere. He started his coaching career in 1985, and eventually it brought him back to the Lions. He retired from coaching after the 1996 season.

65 Mel Gray Puts On a Show

They say big players come up big in big games. That includes return specialists like Mel Gray.

Back on October 23, 1994, the Lions were playing the Chicago Bears. Lions special teams had been under heavy criticism for lack of production. In that game, Gray returned a kickoff from Chris Gardocki 102 yards to tie the all-time Detroit franchise record.

The Bears special teams coach said it was not like they weren't prepared. They knew what they faced in Gray who had been to the Pro Bowl in 1990, 1991, and 1992 and would return in 1994. Gray said the Bears were trying to pin them in corners all day. They had run sideline returns most of the game when Gray went to special teams coach Steve Kazor and told him a middle return would be good because they were flowing to the outside.

Boom! His next return was for 102 yards and a score.

Before coaching Lions' special teams, Kazor had done the same job with the Bears. And he said that prior to playing Detroit, he never slept thanks to the shifty Mel Gray.

While Gray spent a dozen years in the NFL, six of his most productive seasons came with the Lions from 1989–94. In that stretch he played 84 games and returned 216 kickoffs for 5,478 yards, a 25.4 yards per return average. He also returned five kickoffs for touchdowns.

Gray also returned 132 punts for 1,427 yards and two touchdowns. That's an average of 10.8 yards per punt return. In comparison eight punt returners in the 2011 season averaged more than that, including Green Bay's Randall Cobb at 16 yards per return, New England's Julian Edelman at 14, and San Francisco's Ted Ginn at 11.5.

Gray remains the Lions' all-time leader in kickoff returns, career kickoff return yards, career kickoff returns for touchdowns, most kickoff returns for touchdowns in a single season (three in 1994), highest kickoff return average (28.36 in 1994), and career punt return yards.

In his six seasons with the Lions, they went to the playoffs three times and actually won a playoff game in 1991.

In that 1991 season, the Lions were 10–4 and aiming for the NFL Central title when they found themselves in a close game at Green Bay on December 15. Detroit was clinging to a 14–10 lead when Gray put the game out of reach with his longest punt return for the Lions, a 78-yarder for a touchdown with 4:40 to play in the game. The Packers scored again, but thanks to Gray the Lions won 21–17. Through the 2011 season, the Lions have not won at Green Bay since that day.

Gray also holds another mark of distinction. He's the oldest player to return a kickoff for a touchdown at 33 years and 276 days. He's also the second and third oldest in the same category. Gray, who arrived in Detroit in 1989, the same year as Barry Sanders, is considered one of the greatest return specialists of all time in the NFL.

He was named to the NFL's 1990s all-decade team and was ranked fifth on the NFL's Network's top 10 return aces list.

He was drafted by New Orleans in the second round (42nd overall) in the 1984 supplemental draft of USFL and CFL players. He played college ball at Purdue where he was a running back. Gray played high school ball at Lafayette High School in Williamsburg, Va., with future NFL players Lawrence Taylor and Ron Springs.

Gray played for the Saints from 1986 to 1988 before signing with the Lions. After Detroit he played for the Houston/Tennessee Oilers and Philadelphia Eagles, hanging up the cleats after 12 years in the NFL. He had started his football career in the USFL and spent two seasons there.

66 Spielman a Throwback

On game day Chris Spielman, the Lions linebacker, would arrive at the stadium four hours early. He'd drink cup upon cup of coffee. He would stuff smelling salts up his nose. He'd get himself in a very bad mood. Once on the field, he'd take that anger and use it against opponents. It worked.

It's quite possible Chris Spielman was the toughest Lion ever.

And he still is. Spielman left football in 1998 for a year to help take care of his wife Stefanie and their four children early during her fight against breast cancer. Stefanie Spielman fought through five bouts of breast cancer before she died on November 19, 2009, at the age of 42.

Spielman still speaks on her behalf to raise money for the Stefanie Spielman Comprehensive Breast Center at Ohio State University.

Cancer may be the only opponent that Spielman hasn't defeated, but he's not done trying.

While Stefanie was fighting the insidious disease, she was very public about what she was going through. In turn, she received tremendous support from people she didn't know. Her mailbox would be overflowing with good wishes, and mostly it came because her husband had a high-profile career with the Lions and then with the Buffalo Bills for two seasons.

She felt that she was given a platform to make a difference in someone's life, and she used it.

Chris Spielman, who is now an ESPN analyst for college football, is fondly remembered in Detroit for his toughness, his hard work and success on the field.

In his eight seasons in Detroit (1988–95), Spielman missed just four games, all in the 1990 season. He started every game after he was drafted 29th overall by the Lions.

Spielman can best be described as a throwback player, fitting well in another era of football. Spielman, who wore No. 54, is Detroit's all-time leader in career tackles with 1,138. During his Lions career he had 10 sacks, four interceptions, 13 forced fumbles, and 17 fumble recoveries. For his efforts he was the team's defensive MVP in 1993 and 1994 and went to the Pro Bowl four times (1989–91, 1994).

Using the throwback theme, ESPN once introduced a feature on Spielman in black-and-white with Tom Jackson wearing a reporter's fedora, typing on an antique typewriter in what looked like an old-time newspaper office. (It was actually the sports office at *The Oakland Press* in Pontiac, just down the street from the Silverdome.)

Spielman was so tough that in 1995 he suffered a severely torn pectoral muscle in the opening game and played through it.

Linebacker Chris Spielman (54) during a 17–10 loss to the Los Angeles Rams on September 11, 1988, at Anaheim Stadium in Anaheim, California.
(AP Photo/NFL Photos)

After that season, even though he had a doctor's report that said he would get back to 100 percent healthy, he was an unrestricted free agent who got no nibbles from the Lions because of his health.

So he signed with the Buffalo Bills. When he did so, Spielman said, "I have no regrets. They don't owe me a thing. There's emotion but not bitterness."

And then one of the Lions' best shuffled off to Buffalo.

Spielman later proved again and again that he indeed had no bitterness, returning to Detroit occasionally for the annual Courage House Dinner fund-raiser. It seems he's still a Lion at heart.

67 Dick "Night Train" Lane

After four years serving in the army, Dick Lane stopped by the Los Angeles Rams looking for work. Not just any job, though, he wanted to play football. He had played in high school and junior college, so he had experience.

Luckily someone at the Rams was smart enough to give him a shot. At first he was tried out at receiver. Once he was moved to defense, he found a home.

While in Los Angeles, Lane was hanging out with teammate Tom Fears, who continually played the Buddy Morrow song "Night Train." When another teammate found Lane in a room with the music playing, he gave Lane the nickname and it stuck.

It didn't take Lane a long time to adjust to the NFL. He set an NFL record with 14 interceptions in his rookie season, which was 12 games long.

Knee Deep in Texans

There's not a direct pipeline of players making their way from Texas to the Lions, it just seems like it.

Five Lions on the All-Time team played college football in Texas.

They include QB Bobby Layne (Texas), S Yale Lary (Texas A&M), RB Doak Walker (Southern Methodist), G Harley Sewell (Texas), and DT Doug English (Texas).

Also Dick "Night Train" Lane (Austin) and Billy Sims (Hooks) played high school ball in Texas.

Newcomers with Texas connections include QB Matthew Stafford (Highland Park), TE Brandon Pettigrew (Tyler), CB Chris Houston (Austin), T Jason Fox (Fort Worth), C Dylan Gandy (Harlingen, Texas Tech) and LS Don Muhlbach (Lufkin, Texas A&M).

After the Rams, Lane played for the Chicago Cardinals and then the Lions from 1960 to 1965. In that stretch he had 21 interceptions for 272 yards and a touchdown. He played a prominent role in the book, *Paper Lion*.

He was a hard-hitter, and he liked to tackle opponents about the head and neck, which was legal back then. It was called a "Night Train Necktie."

He had speed, agility, and the fierce determination to succeed.

In 1969 he was named the best cornerback of the first 50 years of professional football.

In his career he had 68 interceptions for 1,207 yards, five touchdowns, and 11 fumble recoveries. He earned seven trips to the Pro Bowl, three times while with the Lions. He was All Pro four times and was named to the NFL's All-Decade team for the 1950s.

He received the ultimate honor when he was inducted into the Pro Football Hall of Fame in 1974.

Lane was No. 19 on *The Sporting News'* list of 100 Greatest Football Players. He was the highest rated defensive back on the list and the second highest-ranked Lions player after Barry Sanders.

Perhaps the most unique list you'll find Lane's name on is the NFL Networks' Top 10 undrafted players.

Lane was married three times, and one of his wives was famous jazz singer Dinah Washington. He was her eighth husband, and they were still married at the time of her death.

Perhaps two of Lane's Lions teammates knew him best.

Lem Barney once said, "Train will always be the Godfather of cornerbacks. He was as large as some linemen of his era. He also was agile and very fast. His tackling was awesome. He did the clothesline and other tackles that just devastated the ballcarrier."

Hall of Famer Joe Schmidt said, "Train had great size and speed. I have never seen anyone with the type of closing speed on a receiver that he had. Train took pride in getting to the receiver and making the tackle. He also was a true team player. Whatever he did, he did it for the team."

Former New York Giants kicker and Lions defensive end Pat Summerall said, "I played with him and against him, and he was the best I've ever seen."

Lane was born in Austin, Texas, and raised by Ella Lane, who found him abandoned as an infant.

Lane had a few tough breaks in his life right from the start, but he took advantage of the opportunities presented to him.

68 Green Bay Sent Packing

In Lions history, there are Thanksgiving games and then there are huge Thanksgiving games.

The 1962 Turkey Day matchup against the undefeated Green Bay Packers still stands as one of the biggest games in Lions history—not Thanksgiving history but franchise history.

The Packers, riding a 10–0 streak, arrived in Detroit to play in the annual Thanksgiving game at Tiger Stadium.

The Lions were waiting. They were no pussycats, this bunch. They owned an 8–2 record and their defensive front was one of the best in the game, if not *the* best.

The Lions were hungry that day. They sacked quarterback Bart Starr 11 times. They also intercepted him twice and recorded a safety for good measure. That Thanksgiving the Lions handed the Packers their only loss of the season, a 26–14 drubbing, on national television.

It was the only game the Packers would lose that season.

Three members of that 1962 Lions team—defensive tackle Roger Brown, Hall of Fame linebacker Joe Schmidt, and wide receiver Gail Cogdill—remember that Thanksgiving well.

Their memories are so clear you'd swear they played the game yesterday instead of 50 years ago on November 22, 1962.

"It was a formidable team, and we had respect for them and so forth, but we all felt we had a better football team," Schmidt said.

The Packers were so formidable that they featured 10 future Hall of Famers, including Bart Starr, fullback Jim Taylor, right tackle Forrest Gregg, linebacker Ray Nitschke, cornerback Herb Adderley, defensive end Willie Davis, center Jim Ringo, halfback Paul Hornung, safety Willie Wood, and defensive tackle Henry Jordan. Oh, and they were coached by a guy named Vince Lombardi.

Ahh, but the Lions had a score to settle. They had played and lost to the Packers 9–7 earlier that season at Green Bay.

"The first game we played, [quarterback] Milt Plum gets blamed for throwing the ball, but that came from upstairs to throw the ball," Schmidt said. "We were on our own 45-yard line, it was third down and 7, [and] we were winning 7–6."

Because of the rain, the Lions' receiver slipped and the ball was intercepted, which set up the game-winning field goal for the Packers.

"We always felt we were a better football team. I never to this day can prove that, because the Packers won the championship," Schmidt said.

That loss set up the Thanksgiving rematch.

"I know back in '62 we had a vendetta, we had a game to make up for. Green Bay came in undefeated. We gave them a gift up in Green Bay. We wanted to set the record straight. We had a vendetta against them, and it was hard," Brown said.

They knew that loss should have never happened.

"When Thanksgiving finally came around, it was like, 'Yeah, it's here.' I remember that I never said a word the whole week," Cogdill said. "I don' think the offense did, or defense, they were working toward what it's going to take to do this.

"I remember when we got into the game, I always ran the square end patterns, the square out patterns, the comebacks and stuff, on the particular play that was called, I just told Milt Plum I'm going straight. I believe the defense had really planned on me doing my cuts and stuff into the middle, I did it twice in a row I think we kind of caught them off-guard. I went to the sideline and said, 'Yes, we've got it.' It's like when you're playing cards and you know you have the best hand. It was an awesome feeling that we knew we could take Green Bay that day...to go from there and have it be remembered after all these years I think I played one of the great games, and I enjoyed it," added Cogdill, who had two touchdown catches of 33 and 27 yards that Thanksgiving.

Still, it's a game remembered more for the Lions' defensive whipping of Starr and the Packers' offense.

"Roger [Brown] should be in the Hall of Fame, but for some reason he's not. That particular day he was throwing those people around like toys. We had a defense set up by Don Shula who was our defensive coordinator," Schmidt said.

"They were a good football team, well coached, but I think we were as good or better," he added.

Detroit's defense blitzed like it never had previously. Brown said it was all motivation.

"We did all kinds of nutty things, but we were determined to get to Bart Starr, and I don't think the German Luftwaffe could have stopped us that day," Brown said.

Eleven sacks is a boatload even by today's standards.

"I don't think, 11 sacks in a game, I don't recall any team that had that type of impact on the offense of a football team that we did," Schmidt said. "It could be my statistics are wrong or my thinking is wrong, but at this particular time that's how I feel about it."

The defensive pressure caused the Packers' offense to lose its poise. And then the game.

Years later it's still a good Thanksgiving story—for Lions' fans perhaps more than for Cheeseheads.

The old guys from 1962 are keeping an eye on the 2012 Lions.

Does Brown consider Ndamukong Suh a dirty player?

"I'm going to tell you I'm proud of him and I'm proud that [Suh] plays that tackle spot. I could never get anybody to call me dirty when I played even if I threw dirt in someone's face," Brown said.

"A football player, especially on that defensive line, you're not playing tiddlywinks, this is football. As long as he doesn't try to break somebody's arm or pile on after the whistle blows, that's dirty.

"Suh is doing a heck of a job. I would like to have 22 of them on my team, call them all dirty. I'll tell you what, we'd go right to the Super Bowl," Brown said.

On the other side of the ball, like the rest of the NFL, these guys have noticed wide receiver Calvin Johnson.

"I think what do you want to call it, he's an absolute stud. The guy is awesome. I think he's one of the great weapons the Lions have…. He's the type of person if I was the quarterback, I would have no problem throwing it to him all the time. He's a wonderful athlete," Cogdill said.

Schmidt takes it a step further.

"I'd throw the ball to him every down. He's phenomenal. He has the ability of a basketball player on a football field," Schmidt said. "He can jump, he has tremendous hands, he has tremendous ability to locate the football. He's got excellent speed, he looks like a pretty fast guy. His size is the big thing."

In 2011 the Lions (7–3) had the chance to make history repeat itself when the 10–0 Packers came to Ford Field on Thanksgiving to face the Lions. But it wasn't meant to be, and the Lions fell 27–15.

69 Playoff Highs and Lows

Mention the word "playoffs" to Lions fans and they either groan or giggle. They groan because of the lack of success throughout the years. They giggle when you mention Lions and playoffs in the same sentence. But that's all starting to change.

Let's take a look at the Lions' rich playoff history. You may not realize they won four championships back in the day. In just their second year of existence, in 1935, the Lions beat the New York Giants 26–7 for their first NFL championship. This is before it was called the Super Bowl.

Perhaps it was beginner's luck because it took another 17 years for the Lions to capture their next title. That came on December 28, 1952, when the Lions beat the six-time defending champion Cleveland Browns 17–7 in Cleveland. Bobby Layne was the quarterback, but the running game (258 rushing yards) was the key. So was the Detroit defense that allowed the Browns inside the Lions' 20 just four times.

It was back-to-back championships for the Lions who beat the Browns again on December 27, 1953, with Layne at the helm.

Can you say dynasty?

On December 28, 1957, the Lions won their fourth NFL championship over Cleveland 59–14. Layne was out with a leg broken in three places, so Tobin Rote started in his place. He threw for four touchdowns and ran for another. For the Browns, future Hall of Famer Jim Brown had 20 carries for 69 yards and a score.

Now back to the more recent past.

No more championships. In fact, since that 1957 championship, the Lions have had one playoff win and that came on January 5, 1992.

Let's take a look at the Lions during the modern era of the playoffs:

- 1970 NFC Divisional Playoff game (December 26, 1970): Dallas Cowboys won 5–0 in a game where the Lions' defense allowed 207 rushing yards with 135 of them from Duane Thomas. Lions quarterback Greg Landry was 5-of-12 for 48 yards. Detroit was held to 156 total yards in the shutout at the Cotton Bowl.

- 1982 NFC First-Round Playoff game (January 8, 1983): Washington Redskins won 31–7. Lions quarterback Eric Hipple completed 22-of-38 for 298 yards, one touchdown, and a pair of interceptions. The Lions were down 24–0 at the half and held scoreless until the third quarter in the game at RFK Stadium.

- 1983 NFC Divisional Playoff game (December 31, 1983): The San Francisco 49ers won 24–23. The Lions were down 17–9 at the end of the third quarter, and then Billy Sims scored two rushing touchdowns (11 yards and 3 yards) in the fourth as the Lions took the 23–17 lead. Joe Montana threw the game-winning 14-yard touchdown pass to Freddie Solomon at Candlestick Park.

Scarlet and White

Did you know at one point the Lions changed their colors? It didn't last, though. Their original uniforms from 1934–47 were silver and Honolulu blue. Then in 1948 Alvin "Bo" McMillin was hired as head coach, and he added scarlet and white to the equation because he had come from Indiana and it resembled the colors worn by his Hoosier teams. The jersey was scarlett with white numbers, and the pants were white with a thick black stripe between two scarlett stripes. They also had an all-black uniform that was worn only for important games. The scarlett, white, and black uniforms were mixed and matched. In 1949, they returned to wearing Honolulu blue and silver at home with the combinations of scarlet on the road.

In 1950, they finally went back to wearing blue and silver, ditching the scarlet and white.

- 1991 NFC Divisional Playoff game (January 5, 1992): Lions won 38–6 over Dallas. In one of Erik Kramer's best games, he was 29-of-38 for 341 yards, three touchdowns (two to Willie Green, one to rookie Herman Moore), and zero interceptions. Barry Sanders ran 12 times for 69 yards, including a 47-yard touchdown run in the fourth at the Silverdome. Steve Beuerlein was replaced by Troy Aikman in the Lions' last playoff win.

- 1991 NFC Championship game (January 12, 1992): Redskins won 41–10. The Lions were down 17–10 at the half, but were held scoreless. Erik Kramer was 21-of-33 for 249 yards, one touchdown (to Willie Green), and one interception. Barry Sanders was held to 44 yards on 11 carries. Mark Rypien was 12-of-17 for 228 yards with two touchdowns at RFK Stadium.

- 1993 NFC First-Round Playoff game (January 8, 1994): Green Bay won 28–24. Barry Sanders had one of his best playoff games with 169 yards on 27 carries. Erik Kramer's two interceptions were costly. The Lions held a 24–21 lead in the fourth, but Brett Favre came back with his third touchdown pass of the game—this one to Sterling Sharpe for 40 yards—for the game-winner at the Silverdome.

- 1994 NFC First-Round Playoff game (December 31, 1994): The Packers won 16–12. It may be hard to imagine, but Barry Sanders had 13 carries for minus–1 yards in the game at Lambeau Field. Lions quarterback Dave Krieg was 17-of-35 for 199 yards and a touchdown, but he was no match for Brett Favre who was 23-of-38 for 262 yards.

- 1995 NFC First-Round Playoff game (December 30, 1995): Eagles won 58–37. The Lions were outscored 31–0 in the second quarter. End of story. Oops, just kidding. Lions quarterback Scott Mitchell, who had completed a record-setting regular season, was just 13-of-29 for 155 yards with a touchdown and four interceptions. Barry Sanders ran 10 times for 40 yards. Eagles quarterback Rodney Peete (sound familiar?) threw for three touchdowns at Veterans Stadium.

- 1997 NFC First-Round Playoff game (December 28, 1997): Buccaneers won 20–10. The Lions were down 20–0 in the third. They got on the scoreboard with a 33-yard Jason Hanson field goal and a 1-yard touchdown run by fullback "Touchdown" Tommy Vardell. Scott Mitchell threw for 78 yards and an interception before being hauled off the field on a stretcher. He was replaced by Frank Reich. Quarterback Trent Dilfer got the job done for the Bucs at Houlihan's Stadium.

- 1999 NFC First-Round Playoff game (January 8, 2000): Redskins won 27–13. It was never a contest. The Lions were down 27–0 at the start of the fourth after two rushing touchdowns by Stephen Davis and a touchdown pass from Brad Johnson to Albert Connell. Lions quarterback Gus Frerotte was 21-of-46 for one touchdown and two interceptions. Fullback Cory Schlesinger was the Lions' leading rusher with seven carries for 23 yards.

70 Plimpton's Folly

First of all, if you've never read *Paper Lion* by the late George Plimpton, I have one question for you: What's taken you so long?

It took this book project to get me to order *Paper Lion*. I'm so glad I did. I savored every word. It's a treasure for any Lions' fan or actually any NFL fan. Everyone knows the premise of the book, which was also turned into a movie, but it's the details that make it a literary classic. It's the war stories that George Plimpton was able to put so eloquently into words that make you feel like you were in the training camp dorm (at Cranbrook in Bloomfield Hills), listening to them being told first-hand. Tons of them. And this Lions bunch, like most any NFL team, was filled with characters, including Alex Karras.

Plimpton had a tough time finding an NFL team that would allow him to infiltrate the walls during training camp. He wanted to be at the meetings, on the field doing drills and hanging out with the guys—and sometimes the coaches.

It took a few tries, and then he hooked up with Lions' coach George Wilson who agreed to let Plimpton be his last-string quarterback and to see action in a live intra-squad scrimmage.

Plimpton, who at the time was editor of the *Paris Review*, had done a similar stint in baseball with pitching in an All-Star exhibition. Those experiences were chronicled in *Out of My League*.

His attention to detail makes the book quite the page turner. Before I cracked it open, I didn't think of it as a history book. Plimpton goes into detail with the Lions he played with, including Joe Schmidt, Yale Lary, Milt Plum, Wayne Walker, and Dick "Night Train" Lane, among others.

At first no one knew that Plimpton was a writer, but once he was recognized because of his baseball efforts, word got out. The players had probably wondered why he was always carrying a notebook. It wasn't to write down plays, he was recording details for the book, which became a classic sports book, when it was published.

Plimpton was not afraid to spill his guts about the challenges he faced, either. One of the first was getting used to putting on a helmet and letting it slide over his ears. During the camp workouts he learned five basic offensive plays.

The highlight, as it turns out, was during a team scrimmage under the lights at Wisner Stadium in Pontiac. The 36-year-old Plimpton was the quarterback for the first five plays. It didn't exactly work the way he had envisioned after all his practices. In those five plays, he lost about 30 yards but didn't get seriously injured, which was a plus.

After that night the coach gave him a different type of assignment by putting him in charge of the rookie show, an annual event with skits making fun of veterans and coaches, featuring a little music and an opening with the first-year linemen wearing only jockstraps and high kicking in "a thunderous can-can."

Plimpton's goal was to get in a real preseason game. While he got close, he never made it. The NFL commissioner, Pete Rozelle, didn't want him in and so neither did Lions general manager Edwin Anderson. Still, Plimpton was on the bench for the game, wearing his No. 0. It makes for a perfect photo for the book's cover.

His experiences with the Lions so endeared him to the group he would meet up with them occasionally and would always follow their scores, which wasn't as easy to do then as it would be now. He tells a great story of catching up with some of the Lions in Los Angeles the year after his stint. They wanted to dine at La Scala, a widely popular restaurant, but the place wouldn't take his reservation until he used the name "Bill Ford." That night when he and a few players got to the restaurant, Plimpton was told there was someone who would like to meet him. It was the real William Clay Ford. Oops.

Another time the Lions asked Plimpton to be their representative at the NFL draft in New York. It was an honor but at the same time grueling work. That night he also got back in touch with Mr. Ford, the real one.

Plimpton shared many laughs in the book but also some insights that could only come from an NFL player in the 1960s. It was a different time. And the way Plimpton tells it, you would swear you were there.

The movie version came out in 1968, featuring Alan Alda as Plimpton and Lauren Hutton as his girlfriend, Kate, who was not mentioned in the book. Hey, it was Hollywood. Like all movies based on a book, but there were changes made to amp up the excitement for the big screen.

A number of Lions players were featured in the movie as themselves, including Alex Karras, Joe Schmidt, Roger Brown, Mike Lucci, John Gordy, and Pat Studstill.

I thought the book might be hard to find because it was first published in 1965. However, I was able to order the 40th anniversary edition online at a reduced price.

71 Breaking the Vikings' Curse

Odds were that one day the Lions would break the Vikings curse. While Detroit had taken care of business against Minnesota on home turf, the Lions lost 13 straight at the Metrodome from 1998–2010.

It's an extremely loud and decrepit stadium full of fans who proudly dress like Vikings—enough so that sometimes you wonder: Just how old are their costumes? Are they costumes at all? Where do they park their ships?

Still, 13 years is a long time.

That all changed on September 25, 2011. The Lions were down 20–0 at the half but roared back to win 26–23 in overtime,

Calvin Johnson catches a pass over Minnesota Vikings cornerback Cedric Griffin (23) during overtime of a game on Sunday, September 25, 2011, in Minneapolis. The Lions won 26–23. (AP Photo/Jim Mone)

forcing Vikings fans to drown their sorrows in glog or whatever it is they might drink. It was the third straight win for the Lions.

Afterward, quarterback Matthew Stafford said, "I feel unbelievably unsore right now."

That was despite the fact he had been sacked five times by the beefy and unrelenting Minnesota defense. Perhaps it had something to do with the outcome of the toughest game many of the Detroit Lions said they have ever been involved in.

Down 20–0, Stafford connected with Calvin Johnson on key plays, the Lions took control and finally snapped the curse. With that win, the Lions started the season 3–0 for the first time since 1980.

The Vikings, who dropped to 0–3, had been outscored 67–6 in second-half action over three games.

After digging a 20-point first-half deficit, the Lions did not panic. That's the difference between these Lions and those of yesteryear. No yelling and screaming at half-time. Instead, there was a discussion of how to get back on track.

"It's different, there's enough talent in this room [that] nobody has to yell…. Belief is unreal in here, perseverance. We've been through everything, we've been to hell and back," center Dominic Raiola said. "You been 0–16? Yeah, I've been 0–16, Calvin's been 0–16. Can you get worse than that? No."

It makes a 20–0 deficit seem surmountable. And it was.

It took all 46 Lions, but the win wouldn't have happened without Stafford connecting with Calvin Johnson, starting the scoring in the third quarter on a 32-yard touchdown play.

"Getting our first touchdown to Calvin going down the field, that was a big boost for us," Coach Jim Schwartz said.

Those seven points were big for the offense and sparked the defense, too.

"We knew we had to start somewhere, what a better way to start than the best in the game. Matthew gave him a chance, and he made a big play—it started everything," Raiola said.

The two also connected on the first play in the fourth quarter on a five-yard pass, closing the gap to 20–17. That drive included a 60-yard screen pass to Jahvid Best and a 17-yard completion to Titus Young on a third-and-8.

Perhaps Johnson's biggest play—and it's difficult to rank them (seven catches, 108 yards)—was a 40-yard catch in overtime that set up Jason Hanson's 32-yard game-winning field goal.

It took a village on that play, too.

"It was unbelievable…. Jahvid picked up Chad Greenway right through the middle, he got run over but he gave me enough time to get it off," Stafford said. "Guys stuck in there, [Best] blocked tough all game."

Stafford (32-of-46, 378 yards, two touchdowns) was not the only one who had trouble finding words to describe Johnson.

"Calvin just does his thing. I don't know what to tell you, I can't explain it, he's an unbelievable player," Stafford said. "I just try to give him some chance on balls, and he makes me look really good."

Johnson was one-on-one on that play and Stafford had the confidence to throw it up-field to him.

"You have to trust Calvin to make that play, I think a lot of that comes from the other guys making plays," Schwartz said. "They don't get out of Cover 2 and give us one on one unless Titus is making a play down the seam, unless Brandon Pettigrew keeps making plays, unless Jahvid Best goes 80 yards on the screen or whatever it is [60 actually]."

And no matter what the offense did in the second half, it wouldn't have mattered if the defense hadn't clamped down, holding the Vikings to a 49-yard field goal and 108 total yards in the second half. Of course, that field goal tied it with 9 seconds remaining. But the Lions' offense, which had 308 second-half yards compared to 50 in the first half, wasn't shaken.

"I think we knew we were going to go down there and score, that's the way every good offense is," Stafford said. "We didn't blink at all. We just went down there and put some points on the board, [Jason] Hanson knocked down a field goal like he always does and we got out of here."

If ever there was a game that was different in both halves, it was this one.

"It wasn't really any key adjustments, it was moreso just doing your job," linebacker DeAndre Levy said. "Early on, speaking defensively, a lot of guys were trying to do maybe too much, worrying about 28 [Adrian Peterson] too much.... Once we settled in and did our job, we took away some of those gaps, some of those lanes."

Basically the message at half-time was just do your job, do it the best you can, one play at a time, and probably a few more well-worn cliches.

"We have good players, we have good schemes, we just needed to settle down," Schwartz said. "The worst thing we could do was throw gasoline on the fire. We have a lot of confidence in this team, a lot of confidence that if we were in a slump and if we were going to break out, you don't get out of slumps by doing something different. You go to bread and butter, and you keep on playing."

Bread and butter—aggressive defense and an offense full of weapons with a quarterback who can get them the ball.

It wasn't just Xs and Os that got the Lions the win. Bread and butter is good, but belief in yourself and your teammates is better.

72 Location is Everything

It's hard to miss the Elwood Bar & Grille. It's literally sandwiched between Ford Field and Comerica Park, home of the Detroit

Tigers. And then there's the fact that its Art Deco signature design makes it a standout wherever it might be located.

The Elwood owners advertise that it is so close to the action that you can hear the crack of the bat—and they're not kidding. You can't hear the chorus of "Gridiron Heroes" from Lions' games, but that's only because Ford Field is not an open-air stadium.

Downtown Detroit's most recognizable Art Deco diner was built in 1936 by Detroit architect Charles Noble. It was named after the original location at the corner of Elizabeth Street and Woodward Avenue. El(izabeth)wood(ward). Get it?

In 1997 the Elwood Bar & Grill was saved and moved by its owner Chuck Forbes to 300 Adams Avenue, at the corner of Brush Street, to make way for Comerica Park. It now makes its home right behind left field. It's also just across Brush Street from Ford Field.

Stand inside the Elwood and look through the window across Brush, and you almost feel like you're inside Ford Field.

After the move, the restaurant underwent a complete restoration, including remodeling the art deco interior and renovation of its unique enameled steel facade.

When the weather agrees, there are plenty of outdoor picnic tables set up.

The price of beer is reasonable, and the menu routinely receives good reviews.

It includes a Ty Cobb salad, classic Elwood Detroit Coney with chili and onions, homemade mac and cheese, the Elwood classic all-American burger, nachos, chili, appetizers, and a full list of sandwiches, including an Elwood Cuban with pulled pork, ham, Swiss cheese, pickles, and wasabi aioli on a hoagie bun.

73 Famous Detroiters Big Fans

On December 26, 2010, the Lions had just come back from a rare road victory against the Dolphins in Fort Lauderdale. Reporters were gathered around a podium outside the visiting locker room, waiting to talk to Coach Jim Schwartz when we heard whooping and hollering and a few unprintable words as a certain guest stormed into the winning locker room.

Then minutes later the scent of a victory cigar seeped into the press room.

At that point there was no question who the special guest was—it was Kid Rock who has not only become a fan of Jim Schwartz's but a friend, too.

After the Detroit home opener in the 2011 season, the Lions were 2–0. It was early, but it was a good start. They had beaten Tampa on the road and now Kansas City at Ford Field.

This wasn't lost on some of the local celebrities who are diehard Lions' fans.

Put Kid Rock at the top of the list.

There he was in the locker room, celebrating the 2–0 start with rock 'n' roll legend Bob Seger, another longtime Detroiter and Lions' fan.

Kid Rock, who lives in the northern suburbs, is one of Detroit's best ambassadors.

He's also a big fan of every major sports team in Detroit. He's become friends with a few of the Lions players. It's not unusual to see him celebrating in the locker room.

Bob Seger, who also lives in Oakland County, is not a usual in the locker room. In fact, one of the young reporters was shooting video of Kid Rock talking to the media, and he kept trying to get the old guy out of the frame. His editor informed him the next day that the old guy happened to be Seger. That day they were attending with Uncle Kracker.

In the 2010 season, Kid Rock was given a game ball by Schwartz after a win in which Kid Rock (Bob Ritchie in real life) had treated a few hundred veterans to game tickets.

Kid Rock also filmed the video that honors homegrown soldiers at every Lions game at Ford Field.

Actor Tim Allen, a native Detroiter, has been at Lions' games throughout the years. He was back on Thanksgiving in 2011.

Another actor, Jeff Daniels, usually makes a guest appearance at training camp each summer. He chats with beat writers along the sideline. The first time he was introduced to Schwartz, you could easily sense a certain awe in the coach about having Daniels on board.

When Daniels' work schedule permits, he attends games at Ford Field. Like Kid Rock and Seger, celebrities who could live anywhere, Daniels—who grew up in the Ann Arbor area—still chooses to live life in Michigan rather than Hollywood.

Sinbad the comedian has also attended Lions' training camp—he showed up one day in 2011.

Who Is That Man in the Hard Hat?

You've seen him at Ford Field, maybe on television, or maybe at the airport. You know the Lions' fan with the hard hat, the bib overall shorts, and black work boots.

His name is Ron Crachiola, aka The Crackman, and not only is he a fan but he was inducted in the Pro Football Hall of Fame as a fan in 2001.

He loves the Lions and their fight song, "Gridiron Heroes." Without much prompting, he'll sing it anywhere even on a plane on the way to or returning from one of the Lions' road games.

Crachiola, who works as a lineman for Detroit Edison, has had a love affair with the Lions since his dad first took him to a game in 1955.

It's not like there's a celebrity on every corner in Detroit, but many of the ones who have grown up Lions' fans and still live in the area seem to gravitate to Ford Field.

Jump in an elevator postgame, and you never know whose shoulders you'll be rubbing. Even a somewhat jaded reporter (that's me) was a little awed to share an elevator ride with Bob Seger and Kid Rock.

74 Playoffs Worth the Wait

It was Christmas Eve 2011 when the Lions clinched their first playoff berth in 12 seasons with a win over San Diego.

It was a thrill for each player, but for Dominic Raiola and Jeff Backus, it was a moment that was 11 years in the making.

Raiola and Backus were drafted in 2001 by the Lions. In their first three seasons, Raiola, the center, and Backus, the left tackle, experienced a total of 10 wins—two in 2001, three in 2002 and a whopping five in 2002.

After that big win over the Chargers on Christmas Eve, the Lions would lose at Green Bay the next week to settle for the No. 6 seed. Still, they were in. Finishing at 10–6, it was the first time the Lions had a winning season since 2000.

It was the first winning season for either Raiola or Backus. That's a lot of losing and a lot of heartache.

"I think being what we've been through, those are hard times, but it makes this time that much sweeter. There's more of an appreciation for what's going on around here right now, especially from guys like us. We've been 0–16, only team in the history," Raiola said.

"We know what it feels like to lose, to be out of playoff contention, to plan vacations, to plan what's going on in January and February. Nobody takes it for granted, especially us. It means a little more," Raiola added.

Raiola is the more vocal of the two who have both been anchors on the Lions' offensive line since shortly after they were drafted.

Three weeks before they clinched the playoff berth, the Lions went to New Orleans and lost to the Saints in a nationally televised Sunday Night football game. They killed themselves with penalties, piling up 11 for 107 yards.

Raiola went on a postgame rant in the locker room that consisted of four words repeated over and over: "Grow the [expletive] up." The message was for his teammates.

The win on Christmas Eve over the San Diego Chargers was the third straight win since Raiola spilled his guts.

He took the podium on Christmas Eve and wasn't exactly sure what to say because he had never been in such a spot. He's a natural in talking to the media on a regular basis, but it's usually from a stool in front of his locker, not a podium.

"I mean to do it like that you know it's awesome. No. 9 [Matthew Stafford] came out to play today, he's been playing well. We're going to the postseason, 11 years, it hasn't really sunk in yet. I don't know how to feel. I've never been there before. Long time coming," Raiola said.

Raiola stepped down from the podium, and he gave waiting quarterback Matthew Stafford a big man hug.

Raiola appreciates the fans perhaps more than most because he knows all they've been through with these Lions because he's been through it, too.

"It was electric from play one. It made it real. We're a prideful city and state. [The fans] love the Lions, and I knew that when I got drafted here," Raiola said. "We laid a lot of eggs, but this makes it all worth it. I've been to the bottom and not necessarily to the top.

We're playing in January, that's new ground for us. Let's go deep, who knows what can happen."

The teammates of Raiola and Backus understood the situation.

"We know the history, they've been a part of some tough squads around here. It means a lot to us as fellow teammates to be a part of it with them," Stafford said.

75 Detroit Winner at Super Bowl XL

The Pittsburgh Steelers weren't the only winners of Super Bowl XL.

The City of Detroit and Ford Field received rave reviews from thousands of media members who had descended on the Motor City.

The Steelers, led by an outstanding performance by MVP Hines Ward (five catches for 123 yards and a touchdown), beat the Seattle Seahawks 21–10 that day.

Cold-weather cities never seem to be a favorite Super Bowl spot for fans and the media mobs. Palm trees or parkas? You be the judge.

Fair is fair, though. Super Bowl XL, held February 5, 2006, was the second Super Bowl held in the Detroit area. The first was Super Bowl XVI held at the Pontiac Silverdome, which was won by the San Francisco 49ers in 1982.

The game was awarded by the NFL in 2000 after the Lions had announced they would build a new stadium in Detroit and two years before the final touches were put on Ford Field.

Instead of ignoring the cold, Super Bowl XL organizers embraced it. A winter festival was held on the streets of downtown Detroit. Media members received Super Bowl mittens and hand warmers as their welcome gifts. The organizers were led by Roger Penske, who headed the Super Bowl XL Host Committee. He and his group left no detail to chance.

The volunteers were genuinely happy to welcome outsiders to Detroit.

Organization is key to keep traffic flowing—literally. The Steelers practiced at the Silverdome and stayed nearby in Pontiac. Steelers fans knew just where to go—the lobby at the Center Pointe Marriott to find their favorite players. Two Detroiters—Jerome Bettis and Larry Foote—made Steelers fans out of Lions' fans who were on the fence.

The Seahawks used the Lions indoor practice facility.

So the venues throughout the week leading up to the game were quite spread out. The NFL Experience was held indoors at the Cobo Center, and the media center at the Renaissance Center satisfied every demand.

Just like the warm-weather cities, the Super Bowl parities were a hot ticket and filled with celebrities who jetted in for the week.

It was rated a success.

The whining and complaining about the cold weather or the city itself, never materialized. It was a shining moment for a city that was struggling to rebuild itself and polish its image.

The Rolling Stones performed "Start Me Up," "Rough Justice," and "(I Can't Get No) Satisfaction" at half-time on a serious stage. Detroiter Aretha Franklin and Aaron Neville, along with Dr. John on piano and a 150-member choir, performed the national anthem.

The crowd of 68,206 set an attendance record that stood through the Lions' 2011 season.

Oh, there was a game, too.

With their win, the Steelers became the first No. 6 seed to win a Super Bowl. They were led by Ben Roethlisberger, whose hometown of Findlay, Ohio, is just 100 miles south of Ford Field. He didn't have a great game—the Steelers almost won despite him—but Big Ben became the youngest Super Bowl–winning quarterback in NFL history at the age of 23. He completed just 9-of-21 passes for 123 yards and two interceptions, his passer rating was an ugly 22.6 the lowest of any Super Bowl winning quarterback. It didn't matter, though, he was a Super Bowl champion.

And so was the city of Detroit, along with Ford Field.

The success of the Super Bowl, the first major sporting event held at Ford Field, led to others like the 2009 NCAA Final Four which drew 145,591, the 2010 NCAA Frozen Four (attendance 72,546), and the 2003 Basketbowl where Kentucky and Michigan State played in front of 78,128.

76 Another Detroit Tradition

Detroit's Thanksgiving parade has it all—huge glitzy floats, marching bands galore, the coolest clowns, the big-head gang, special guests, and of course, the visitor from the North Pole.

It is almost as much of a tradition as the Lions' Thanksgiving game. The parade is 80-plus years old, while the Lions have played on Thanksgiving since 1934 minus a few war-time years. The parade, sandwiched between the early morning Turkey Trot and the Lions kickoff, is produced by the non-profit civic group, The Parade Company.

In 2011 more than 21,000 runners participated in the 5K run. More than 60,000 fans watched the undefeated Green Bay Packers beat up on the Lions. And many Detroiters participated in more than one of the events.

Thanksgiving in Detroit is often cold, and sometimes snowy or rainy, but the Thanksgiving parade always goes on. With good weather in 2011 fans were lined up 10 deep in spots to see the floats, the big heads, and yes, the clowns.

Perhaps the clowns in Detroit are more special than any other parade clowns. That's because under the makeup and clown get-ups, they are corporate presidents, community leaders, and other big-shots. They are know as the Distinguished Clown Corps. To get into the act, they make generous contributions to keep the parade going from year to year. More than 2,000 clowns have been involved in the parade, handing out candy and beads. Everyone loves beads, and no trip to the Mardi Gras is required.

Along with the floats and marching bands, the Big Head Corps has also become a Thanksgiving parade staple.

These are my favorites, even though it's difficult sometimes to identify just which person the big heads represent. Like the clown posse, this is a group of young professionals that don these *papier-mache* heads for a donation. Many of these colorful big heads were originally acquired from artists in Viareggio, Italy, with some dating back to the 1940s. The collection numbers more than 300 pieces and many have been restored by the artists at The Parade Company.

Many Detroit icons have their own big heads. Magic Johnson's big head was introduced in 2011. Others include Bob Seger, Diana Ross, Joe Louis, and Rosa Parks.

The grand marshals each year are among Detroit's leaders. In 2011 it was Bill Ford Jr., vice chairman of the Lions. He rode in a blue Mustang convertible with his wife, Lisa.

And, of course, the special guest is Santa Claus, who brings up the rear.

The parade, which kicks off at 9:00 AM, starts at Woodward Avenue and Mack and ends at Woodward and Congress. At certain areas, parade goers are often 10 deep along the Woodward sidewalks.

It's an event that should be experienced by every Detroiter. Topping it off with the Lions game would make for one great turkey day.

77 Totally Multidimensional

Coach Jim Schwartz would have loved Yale Lary, who was a defensive back, punter, and kick returner for the Lions. Schwartz loves multidimensional players and that exactly describes Lary, who was inducted into the Pro Football Hall of Fame in 1979 and played in nine Pro Bowls.

Lary, a three-sport high school athlete, was a defensive back at Texas A&M. In 1952 he was drafted by the Lions in the third round (34th overall).

Hard to imagine, but pro football was not big in Texas during that era.

"We didn't get much pro ball down here at all," Lary recently recounted for profootballhof.com. "We didn't know much about the draft—didn't really know there was one."

Pro teams would send brochures and questionnaires to the players. Lary remembered that some of the seniors would have fun filling out the questions by writing down exaggerated heights and weights with extremely fast times in the 100-yard dash. (So that's why the NFL eventually came up with the NFL Combine.)

Lary, though, knew the Lions were interested in him because, before the draft, Lions coach Buddy Parker visited Lary and took him to lunch. They discussed the possibility of Lary playing in Detroit.

Lary, who was 5'11" and 185 pounds, played for the Lions from 1952–64 with two years out for army duty in 1954 and '55.

When you talk about Lary, it's not coincidence that he was on the Lions' three championships teams in 1952, 1953, and 1957.

He was the starting right safety, today he would have been the strong safety, for 11 seasons. He finished his career with 50 interceptions, which is still third on the Lions' all-time list. He is also second all-time with career interception return yards with 787. Lem Barney is first with 1,077.

Hall of Fame punter, punt returner, defensive back, and running back Yale Lary of the Detroit Lions. (AP Photo/NFL Photos)

Lary also won punting titles in 1959, 1961, and 1963; he missed it in 1962 by 3.6 inches.

Hall of Famer Paul Hornung said in 2004 that Lary was the best punter ever.

When Lary punted from the end zone, he could put the ball across midfield with enough hang time to give his teammates the chance to cover it. Team captain and linebacker Joe Schmidt said Lary made the defense look good because he gave them room to work.

Lary had just four punts blocked out of 503 in his career. He had a string of six games and 32 punts with no returns.

He's never been forgotten in Detroit. The Lions' annual Special Teams Player of the Year award is named for Yale Lary.

78 Father and Son Lions

Offensive lineman Bob Kowalkowski played the Dallas Cowboys in the Lions' first game at the Silverdome in 1975. In 2001, Bob's son, Scott, a linebacker and special teams player, played the Cowboys in the Lions' final game at the Silverdome. The Kowalkowskis had gone full circle.

Bob and Scott Kowalkowski are believed to be one of two sets of fathers and sons who have played for the Lions. Mel Farr (1967–73) and his son Mike (1990–92) also fall in that category.

"Bob exemplified the tough, physical player you had to be to succeed in the NFL," said Pro Football Hall of Famer Charlie Sanders, who played nine seasons with Kowalkowski. "When you played with him, you knew he had your back, and if he was your friend, he was your friend for life."

Bob Kowalkowski, who died in September 2009, was drafted by the Lions in 1965 and played for 11 seasons (1966–76).

His teammates remembered him as determined to outwork everyone.

Quarterback Greg Landry remembered that Kowalkowski, who was a little undersized compared to most offensive linemen, made up for it with hard work on and off the field.

Kowalkowski had been drafted out of Virginia by the Lions in the fifth round (95th overall) in 1965. After 11 seasons in Detroit, he played his final season with the Green Bay Packers (1977).

His son Scott had been drafted and played three seasons for Philadelphia before signing as a free agent with the Lions in 1994, and he played through the 2001 season. He must have got some of that same toughness from his father because he excelled on special teams where toughness is key. And in his eight seasons with the Lions, Scott missed just two games.

He was also an iron man at the University of Notre Dame where he was the only player who didn't miss a game from 1987–1990. He was an All-American defensive lineman at St. Mary's Prep in Orchard Lake, Michigan.

Bob Kowalkowski was voted the Lions' Man of the Year in 1975 for his community involvement. He had started a golf tournament in 1973 to support Leader Dogs for the Blind. That tournament, the Kowalkowski Open, grew into what is now known as Kolo Charities, which has raised thousands of dollars for a variety of Michigan charities, including the Detroit Lions Courage House, which benefits the child abuse prevention and treatment program at HAVEN in Oakland County.

Still, two Kowalkowskis was not enough for the Lions. Since 1990, Judy Kowalkowski, Scott's mother, has worked as the Lions' manager of accounting operations.

And if that wasn't enough, fullback Brock Olivo, Scott's cousin, played for the Lions from 1998–2001.

79 The Old Ball Games

Lions and Tigers, oh my.

It's a rare double-header, but it happens occasionally that the Lions and Tigers have home games on the same day, at different times. Ford Field and Comerica Park stand shoulder to shoulder in downtown Detroit. They share a parking garage, parking lots, and drinking establishments that cater to both sets of fans.

Because there's not much of a crossover in their seasons, there's little concern about conflicting game schedules. When the Tigers get to the playoffs is the most likely scenario where problems could occur.

During the 2010 and 2011 Lions' preseason, there were concerts at Comerica—one year Eminem, one year Kid Rock—that were ongoing during preseason games.

How close is close?

The concert noise broke through the walls of Ford Field. And afterward, while walking to their cars, Lions fans could clearly hear exactly what was going on at Comerica Park.

It's rare to attend two ball games in one day, though.

So exactly how many hot dogs and beers can one body handle? It's a test you might not want to put your body through too often, but there could be worse things to do to your body (at least I think there could be).

If the Lions won their game, then you could head to Comerica to see what the Tigers could do. It would certainly make for a more enjoyable marathon game day than it would be if the Lions got smacked around.

It would be refreshing to head to Comerica Park, an outdoor baseball shrine, after a day of being inside at Ford Field, one of the NFL's elite stadiums that exudes character and class.

Here's the thing. In a town like Detroit, the athletes spread their wings and become fans of Detroit's teams even if they grew up elsewhere.

Soon after quarterback Matthew Stafford, a native Texan, was drafted by the Lions, he started sporting a Detroit Tigers ball cap. It's his usual headgear. Other Lions are the same, including center Dominic Raiola, who has adopted Detroit after living in the town for more than 10 years. He's a big Red Wings fan, too.

Several of the Lions, including Ndamukong Suh, make their way north to Pistons games. It's mostly one big happy sports family in Detroit. The fans can revel in it.

What a better way to do it than double dip—Lions in the early afternoon and a nightcap at Comerica Park with the Tigers.

There's another opportunity just down the street, too. Many Red Wings players have been in Detroit for years, and they have become Lions fans and vice versa. Now there's another double-dip—Lions game in the early afternoon, Red Wings game in the evening.

There's one more possibility, but it involves considerably more driving. Check out the Lions at 1:00 PM, then drive north up I-75 to the Palace of Auburn Hills and watch the Pistons. Don't even think about the traffic jams. Just make it a special day. It's good to be a Detroiter. It's a good sports town with great sports fans.

80 Gary Danielson's Ups and Downs

Gary Danielson's up-and-down Lions career ended with a seat on the bench for the final game of 1984, a 30–13 loss to the Chicago Bears. It wasn't a statement by Coach Monte Clark; it was a jammed big toe on the quarterback's right foot.

Not a glorious ending to a nine-year career in Detroit.

Danielson didn't know it then, but it would be his final game with the Lions. Actually when that 4–11–1 season was mercifully over, he thought he should be the starter heading into camp for the 1985 season. Instead he was traded to the Cleveland Browns.

Danielson had his best season that year, but the Lions floundered and lost 5-of-6 out of the gate. Four of those early losses were by a total of 11 points.

In seven games that season, Danielson had a quarterback passer rating of 100.0 or more. The only other Lion who has done better is Matthew Stafford, who had 10 games with a passer rating of 100.0 or more.

Danielson was looking to break the records for attempts, completions, and yardage that he had set in 1980. The 1984 season was just the second full season that Danielson had played. In 1978 Danielson threw five touchdowns in a 45–14 win over Minnesota. No other Lions quarterback has topped that mark, although Matthew Stafford has equaled it three times.

That's the odd thing about Gary Danielson and the Lions. In the two seasons (1980 and 1984) that he was the full-time starter, he had his best seasons. In those seasons he threw for 3,223 and 3,076 yards, respectively. He was the Lions third all-time passing leader when he was shipped to Cleveland.

Actually, it's not so odd when it comes to the Lions. They were mostly mired in mediocrity during Danielson's tenure. From 1976 to 1984, the Lions had just two seasons with winning records—9–7 in 1980 and 9–7 in 1983.

They had fallen to 2–14 in 1979 when Danielson was injured in the preseason and missed the entire season.

The Lions had a good quarterback when they had Danielson, a local product who played at Dearborn Divine Child. Some of his Lions records still stand. His final seven years coincided with Monte Clark's tenure as Lions' coach. Clark was fired after the

Gary Danielson (16) passes as San Francisco 49ers defensive end Jeff Stover (72) rushes him and Lions guard Don Greco (67) reaches for Stover in a game at Candlestick Park on Saturday, December 31, 1983. (AP Photo/Al Golub)

1984 season. He had replaced Tommy Hudspeth who went 11–13 in two seasons. During this whole time Russ Thomas was the general manager.

Danielson, who played college ball at Purdue, retired after three seasons in Cleveland. He worked as a college football commentator for years, and these days he's with CBS.

81 All-You-Can-Eat Seats

Everybody looks for a bargain, but it's rare to find one at a concession stand, no matter the sport, no matter the stadium.

Soft drinks cost as much as a case at the grocery store, while hot dogs are tasty but can cost $5 or more. Eating at a game can put a dent in the wallet, a big one. At the same time you can hardly sit in a stadium for several hours without munching on something.

Always looking for a way to attract new fans—and in this case particularly hungry fans—the Lions started selling All-You-Can-Eat seats a few years ago.

The popularity has grown a little each year, with tickets that provide all-you-can-eat hot dogs, nachos, hamburgers, popcorn, pretzels, and soft drinks.

They tweak the menu a bit each year, looking at what's most popular and depending on feedback for what the fans would like to add to the all-you-can-eat menu.

"A famous promotion in the sports world is all-you-can-eat Dodger dogs for a dollar on Tuesdays, that's one of the things we looked at," Lions team president Tom Lewand said.

He won't take credit for the original idea.

"I would be lying if I said it was unique, it's been done in baseball in different places. What we try to do is look at some of the best ideas across the entertainment industry, regardless of whether or not they've ever been applied to the NFL, and use those," Lewand said.

When the Lions were in their lean football years, they had to find new ways to attract football fans to the games. Because at the time, a winning football team just wasn't part of the equation.

"It's again a lot of what we challenged our sales staff to do, particularly during tough times economically in this city and tough

With Sisu from the U.P.

Coming off the 2–14 season in 2009, the Lions felt they could use any good luck charm. They got a live one in Joe Paquette, a longtime Lions fan from Munising in the Upper Peninsula.

Paquette made a 17-day, 450-mile journey, walking from his home to the Lions practice facility in Allen Park, in August 2010 to bring them the message of sisu.

Sisu is, according to *The New York Times*, "the word that explains Finland," and the Finns' "favorite word"—"the most wonderful of all their words."

The literal translation to English is "having guts."

"Sisu is a word in the U.P. Outside of the word 'eh,' it's probably the most recognizable one," Paquette said. "It means persevere, bounce back from a difficult situation, which we all know the Lions are in. I said that's what the Lions need, they need sisu. But how do you get it down there?"

He brought it.

In the 2010 season, the Lions improved to 6–10. No one knows if it was because of the draft that brought Ndamukong Suh, the free agent signings of Kyle Vanden Bosch and Nate Burleson, or the sisu. We report, you decide.

times from a football standpoint, was to look at ways to enhance the entertainment proposition and the value proposition of people making an investment," Lewand said.

"When you can say I can buy these tickets and know that once I walk into the stadium I don't have to shell out another nickel. Or if I'm giving these tickets away to somebody I can know that it's a true gift, take your family down and enjoy the day and you won't have to reach into your pocket for your wallet and it's been very successful."

The all-you-can-eat phenomena could spread into other parts of Ford Field.

When Ford Field hosted Super Bowl XL, they offered per-person pricing in the suites. Once they paid a per-person fee, they could eat all they wanted, including food in the suites and also things such as carved prime rib at community stations.

"It worked really well. Those kinds of things we continue to look at. It's not just the people in the general seating bowl who like the idea of not having to take their wallet out of their pockets... people in the suites and club areas [want] the same thing," Lewand said. "I think you'll see more of those kinds of inclusive opportunities in all parts of the stadium."

82 RIP Tom "Killer" Kowalski

On one of Tom Kowalski's first road trips as a beat writer to cover the Detroit Lions, he wore the new dress shoes he had purchased just for the occasion, a trip to San Francisco. After a night of climbing the hills, exploring the city, and perhaps partaking of a beverage or two, he got back to his room, took off his shoes, and found blisters that had broken and bloodied his socks.

It was his welcome to the NFL road show, which is not as glamorous as it might seem.

Whatever it takes.

Over the years Kowalski grew into a media expert on the Lions. He was just preparing for this 30th season of covering the team when he died of congestive heart failure at age 51 on August 29, 2011.

His death was a huge loss for his fiancée, family, friends, colleagues, the community, and Lions fans everywhere.

He had spread his wings as the media world changed around him. He embraced change and wanted to be among the leaders of the new journalism world that included blogs, video, and Twitter.

He was one of the first to post video blogs showing him voicing his opinion instead of just writing it. He didn't take offense at the criticism—one guy told him he looked like a bloated Hitler—he loved the fact that he was drawing millions of monthly hits to Mlive.com. Bring on the insults, he could take them. He was 6'6" and 300-something pounds.

Kowalski had also hit the sports talk radio airwaves and could jaw with the best of them. His specialty was the Lions, but his love was sports in general.

He was given the nickname "Killer" as a kid after the pro wrestler Killer Kowalski.

Once when doing Detroit radio, Kowalski was followed by comedian Dennis Miller who made some reference to following Killer Kowalski. Tom was proud that Miller had actually said his name.

Opinions? He had a million of them, and it was difficult to change his mind. But it was fun trying.

In doing research for this book, I was going through clips of the 1990 Lions' season when one paragraph jumped off the page. It is classic from Kowalski.

The column was written after the Lions had just beaten the Packers 24–17 at Green Bay (yes, you read that right). It was 2 degrees at game time with a wind chill of minus–33. A perfect day at Lambeau Field.

The Lions tried to give away the game with miscues—a fumble, interceptions, a missed field goal, you name it. Detroit was down 17–10 at the end of the third and came back with two fourth-quarter touchdowns to win.

So Kowalski was telling fans not to feel guilty if a depression came over them in the second half because they thought for sure the Lions would lose.

This is the paragraph as it appeared in *The Oakland Press* on December 23, 1990: "It's conditioning. When the Lions go into a tailspin, we've been conditioned for 30 years to believe they'll never pull it out. To watch a team, or career, crash and burn does not alarm us. We're numbed by it. Oh, missed the playoffs again. Ah, another No. 1 Flop."

It was pure Killer.

He died the morning before a Lions practice. After that session, a visibly shaken Jim Schwartz took the podium and asked for the cameras to be turned off at the start of Monday's post-practice press conference. That was a first.

Kowalski quite often asked the first question of Schwartz. To honor Kowalski, Schwartz left the first question to go unasked, and there was a moment of silence from the media who were all stunned at the heart-breaking news.

"We just brought the team up and had a moment of silence and prayer," Schwartz said. "Obviously our condolences go out to his friends and family, of which we consider ourselves both here.

"I'll just say this about Tom. The one thing he always tried to do was get it right. He knew football, and he always wanted to get it right, and we had a lot of respect for that," the coach said.

Kowalski also had become a mainstay on the FOX 2 Detroit affiliate's pregame show with his keys to the game. Had the coaches listened over the years, perhaps the Lions would have won a few more games. On second thought, perhaps not. On the Christmas Eve pregame show following his death, the hosts and on-air talent each wore one of Kowalski's Jerry Garcia ties, given to them by his fiancée, Diane Wolan.

When he died, condolences poured in from all over the NFL world. Kowalski was a Pro Football Hall of Fame voter, a prestigious task that he took with the appropriate amount of reverence. One of his fellow Hall of Fame voters said he didn't always agree with Kowalski but admits he always had his facts straight and was a great debater.

In Kowalski's last full season on the beat, his editor had suggested he write film reviews of each game. Another task he took so seriously that after offending center Dominic Raiola and the offensive line, Raiola put a tape barrier on the carpet around his locker to keep Kowalski out.

After Kowalski's death, the media rooms at the Detroit Lions practice facility were named for Kowalski.

His friends vowed to keep his charities going and started a foundation in his name.

For a dozen or so Christmases, Kowalski had hosted a fundraiser at a little dive bar in Keego Harbor. He served as a celebrity bartender, and over the years the event grew and grew. In 2011, without Tom, it went on. It wasn't the same, but it was what Tom Kowalski would have wanted.

That's how he's remembered as a generous soul who made friends everywhere.

And years after the bloody socks incident, he had changed to sneakers—always pure white, always perfectly clean. At his memorial service, a pair of his well-worn shoes sat on a folding chair near the podium. So fitting.

On a personal note, Kowalski was my friend and mentor for 30-plus years. He pushed me to better, and he brought out the best in me and the rest of us.

He is missed.

83 25 Years of Brandstatter

In 25 years Jim Brandstatter has experienced the highs and lows of the Lions. Back in the 1990s he watched Barry Sanders work his magic. Then it was on to a decade of despair capped off with the 0–16 season in 2008.

Brandstatter saw the turn-around start in 2009 and move forward through the 2011 season.

Through it all, Brandstatter has called the Lions games on the radio. Twenty-five years makes for many games, more calls, some heartbreak, and the joy in seeing good players on the field wearing the Honolulu blue and silver. Competitive games are the hot fudge for a seasoned radio analyst.

It should be no surprise that the 0–16 season was the most difficult for Brandstatter.

"You had to play games with yourself before every game. How do you broadcast this when going in you know you have little or no chance to win? You've got to be as fired up, as passionate, no matter what," Brandstatter said. "I know what I did. I said, 'Okay, it's a one-game season. It doesn't matter what happens tomorrow, it doesn't matter what happens down the road. All that matters is right now, on this play, do your job as well as you can on this play. When the final score comes out, you've done your job.'"

Success for the Lions makes Brandstatter's job easier.

"Instead of sitting there when you're 0–16 thinking how are we going to cover this guy and we have no chance of stopping him," Brandstatter said. "Now as an analyst—the play-by-pay guy deals with numbers, names, formations, yardages. My job is to figure out how somebody's going to get things done. You can look at games, and you can see match-ups."

He used Lions wide receiver Bill Schroeder (2002–03), who had played at Green Bay, as an example.

"Who cares where he lined up? They could cover him with anybody. When they're covering Mike Williams [wide receiver, 2005–2006] with a linebacker, obviously he didn't have much speed if you're going to cover him with a linebacker."

Now with more talent on the team, Brandstatter said he's like a kid in a candy store.

He's a big fan of Matthew Stafford. For many people, the Cleveland game in Stafford's rookie season, when he went back in the game with a separated shoulder to throw the winning touchdown pass was the clearest indicator that Stafford was the real deal.

"This year [2011] he showed that he's also got it between the ears. He's going to be great for a lot of years if he stays healthy. I like him a lot," Brandstatter said.

Of course he liked Barry Sanders, too. Who wouldn't?

For Brandstatter there are two things that stand out about the Hall of Fame running back. One is how Sanders tore Rod Woodson's ACL and Woodson never touched him.

"He made guys who were All-Pros look silly. Rod Woodson is one of the best corners in the decade. I think it was a preseason game, he came up and made a move on Rod Woodson. Rod Woodson's upper body went one way, and his lower body went the other," Brandstatter said. "He ran by him, and Woodson never laid a glove on him. That's stuff you just don't see every day."

Also he remembers a particular play against Green Bay when Sanders ran a sweep and no one blocked the corner. Sanders just made him miss and went on with his business. All Xs and Os were thrown out with Sanders in the offense.

Sanders was one of the best, but Brandstatter has seen more good football in person than most fans during the last three decades. Not only has he called Lions games for 25 years, he's also worked University of Michigan football games for 30 years.

As you can imagine that makes for some busy weekends and travel headaches. It was especially hard when Brandstatter, who was an offensive tackle at Michigan from 1969–71, used to tape *Michigan Replay* (a highlights show) on Saturday nights after the team got back to Ann Arbor. He had no choice but to fly to the city where the Lions were playing on Sunday morning.

It's amazing that Brandstatter has only been late twice for Lions games. Once was due to snowy conditions and the fact his

Twittering Fools

All the Lions' Twitter activity starts with Coach Jim Schwartz (@Jschwartzlions), who usually tweets his iPod musical selections from the bus on the way to games. Don't get any controversy from him, but we know he's a metal-head.

Twitter has changed the way players interact with the fans. Nate Burleson, Matthew Stafford, Calvin Johnson, Ndamukong Suh, Chris Houston, Titus Young, Chris Harris, and many other players actively tweet. Some more actively than others. Some break news. When there were rumors that Burleson had signed with the Lions as a free agent in March 2010, he confirmed them with a tweet that said, "Hello Detroit."

Cornerback Aaron Berry raised a stink with a tweet after the playoff loss at New Orleans telling certain fans they could go back to being broke and miserable. He apologized and tried to explain himself but it turned out to be a good lesson of why you should not tweet when you're emotional.

cab driver in Minneapolis couldn't go faster than 10 mph. In fact that day, Brandstatter said he did his part of the pregame show on the phone from the cab. He was walking the concourse at the Metrodome, on his way to the radio booth, when he heard the official call the coin toss.

Another time was the Sunday after Michigan played at Ohio State, the day after Bo Schembechler died in 2006. Brandstatter's flight to Phoenix was delayed by mechanical problems, so he arrived two or three minutes late. Curt Sylvester, the Free Press beat writer, was filling in.

"I walked into the booth, no one was more relieved than Curt Sylvester. He looked at me and threw the headset and said, 'Here, take these,'" Brandstatter said.

There was another time he needed to get to Green Bay on a Sunday morning after a late Saturday Michigan game. That's a tough one, there aren't a lot of flights to Cheesehead country. He asked his friend Ron Kramer if he knew a pilot who would fly him to Green Bay in return for four press box passes at Lambeau Field.

Brandstatter got three hours of sleep on a couch at Crisler Arena, made it to Willow Run Airport in Ypsilanti, and then to Green Bay in plenty of time.

It's always a wild fall for Brandstatter who never complains.

He said he's thankful for the friendships he's made in the booth over the years—Frank Beckmann, Mark Champion, and for the last seven years he's worked with Dan Miller calling Lions' games.

"Since we've worked together we've had such great fun, I'm passionate about the game, he's passionate and very prepared," Brandstatter said.

84 History Comes Alive

Where can you see the actual chair that Abraham Lincoln was sitting in at the theater when he was assassinated? Not far away is the bus that Rosa Parks was on when she made headlines because she wouldn't take a back seat.

That's just down a few aisles past the presidential limousines, including the 1961 Lincoln that John F. Kennedy rode in on November 22, 1963, in Dallas.

The Henry Ford Museum in Dearborn honors the tradition of the Motor City with a new 80,000-square-foot display called Driving America, featuring 115 vehicles, some displayed previously others that have been in storage. It's not just cars there's a functioning diner, state-of-the-art theaters, hands-on displays, and the original McDonald's golden arches, an old-fashioned Holiday Inn roadside sign, a Texaco filling station, a Checker cab, and more.

Two of the cars couldn't be more different—there's a 1959 Cadillac Eldorado Biarritz convertible V–8 with a $7,401 list price

A 1952 version of the Oscar Meyer Wienermobile is seen at the Henry Ford Museum in Dearborn, Michigan, on Wednesday, June 28, 2006. Oscar Mayer created the Wienermobile in 1936 to transfer the company spokesperson from store to store. The original was a 13' metal hot dog on wheels with an open cockpit in the center and rear so the hotdogger could pop up. Hog dog whistles were given out starting in 1951, and many people still show up at Wienermobile events looking for the whistles. (AP Photo/Carlos Osorio)

when it was new. Next to it is a 2009 Ford Focus electric car built to promote the 2012 Focus electric car. No price listed on that one.

The museum, however, is about much more than cars. It's clearly a step back in history, a tribute to Americana. It's not just old tractors and steam locomotives—although they are certainly included.

On my visit, the first thing I saw was the Oscar Mayer Wienermobile from 1952. It was the Wienermobile prototype for the Wienermobile fleet built in 1988. It was parked just outside the Wienermobile Cafe. Too funny.

Visit the museum when you've got plenty of time because it will take a while just to get a taste of the offerings. Along with the Wienermobile Cafe, there's Lamy's diner in the Driving America exhibit and the Michigan Cafe. It's easy to see why they offer memberships because one day is just not enough to do it all justice.

Pick your areas and get to it.

One of the sections I found most interesting was the Heroes of the Sky. They had a Ford Flivver, a really small airplane with a wooden propeller built in 1926 at the request of Henry Ford who was hoping it would become the Model T of the sky. He ordered the architect of the plane to make it so small it would fit in his office. When Ford had lost $5.5 million on the Ford aviation division and his test pilot was killed, he gave up the idea.

There were also a few passenger planes, including one with wooden wings—the 1925 Fokker F-VII Trimotor—that had seats for two pilots and 10 passengers. Now, I'm not afraid of flying at all, but you would have never gotten me in one of these contraptions. Holy cow.

They even had a replica of the 1903 Wright Flyer that had an average speed of 9.9 mph. Its longest flight was 852'.

In a glass case, in the With Liberty and Justice for All area, was Abraham Lincoln's chair where he was shot on April 14, 1865. Oddly enough, it's a rocking chair. In that same area there was quite a display on women suffragettes who fought so hard so women could have the right to vote. In the 1800s, women had fewer rights than male inmates in insane asylums. They couldn't vote, serve on a jury, testify in court, hold public office, attend college, or practice law. In 1920 after winning the right, 26 million women voted in the presidential election. Okay, I'll get off my soapbox now.

You can climb on the Rosa Parks bus and listen to a three-minute audio with her explaining what happened that day. The bus is displayed in an area saluting American freedom and equality. The scariest display there is of a Ku Klux Klan fan robe.

Along with the Kennedy presidential limousine, there was the Dwight D. Eisenhower Bubbletop, a 1950 Lincoln with a Plexiglas bubble over the back seat. Very cool. Franklin Delano Roosevelt's Sunshine Special, a 1939 Lincoln, is one of the most elegant pieces in the display. It's a beaut.

In the museum gift shop I found an Abraham Lincoln bobblehead ($24.99)—you don't see those just anywhere. Also Wienermobile paraphernalia including whistles, Hot Wheels, banks, decks of cards, and Christmas ornaments.

Confession, I drive by the Henry Ford entrance at least 100 days a year on my way to cover the Detroit Lions at their practice facility, and don't even think about making a visit. I hadn't been to the museum since I was a kid. I will be making a return appearance, and it will be soon.

85 Angry Man March

It was a blustery mid-December Sunday in Detroit.

After what Lions fans had endured for several years, the cold was not an issue at all.

Before the Lions' final home game of the 2005 season, about 1,000 fans participated in the Angry Man March protesting the five-year extension of the contract of team president and CEO Matt Millen.

The banner that led the march for the five blocks to Ford Field read, "There's a Millen reasons the Lions can't win, 20–57."

Millen's record since he had taken the job in 2001 was 20–57.

The march was organized by radio host Sean Baligian from WDFN, a Detroit sports talk station. Millen was the subject of many hours of sports talk radio in Detroit for too many years.

The march coincided with an "orange out" where fans were asked to wear hunter orange T-shirts, the color of the Cincinnati Bengals, the opponent that day. It was another way fans tried to get the attention of owner William Clay Ford Sr.

The late Tom Kowalski, a longtime Lions beat writer who also worked for WDFN, didn't necessarily agree with the march because he didn't think it would accomplish anything. At the time Kowalski said he was "99 percent certain" Millen would be around for the foreseeable future.

Kowalski also said that while the Lions organization was upset about the march, they weren't that upset. A passionate Lions' fan is better than an apathetic one.

The organizers wanted a peaceful march, and they got it. The Detroit Police Department was prepared and out in force, but made no arrests.

"We want to promote people protesting, showing their feelings in a creative way, and having fun with it," Rona Danziger, programming director at WDFN, told the *Detroit News*. "It's about showing the Lions how fans feel in an organized, peaceful way."

Several hundred fans started the march, and numbers grew to about 1,000 as they approached Ford Field.

They chanted "Fire Millen" and "Ho-ho-ho, Millen must go." They carried signs that said stuff like "Fed Up" and "Commitment to Ineptness."

Fittingly, the Lions lost 41–17 that day on the way to finishing the 2005 season with a 5–11 record.

Millen was fired, but not soon enough for many fans. When he was finally let go, his Lions' record was 31–97. He was fired on September 24, 2008, when the Lions started the season 0–3. Of course they would finish that season setting an NFL mark for futility with an 0–16 record.

The day Millen was fired, sports talk radio again was all abuzz. His firing had taken so long and had come so unexpectedly after just three games in the season, that fans seemed genuinely stunned. And because Millen had the reins for so long, many fans were wary of who would be hired to replace him. Martin Mayhew, who was already on the staff, took the job on the interim basis and then got the job permanently after the season. The Fords seemed to have made a wise choice. Very rarely is Mayhew the subject of radio rants. That means he seems to have the team headed in the right direction.

86 Andolsek Gone Too Soon

When teammate Chris Spielman delivered the eulogy at Eric Andolsek's funeral, he said, "When Eric passed, a piece of me died."

Andolsek, the Lions starting left guard, was whacking weeds around his mailbox at his home west of Thibodaux, Louisiana. His family all lived nearby. When Andolsek wasn't suiting up for the Lions, home is where he wanted to be.

Then on that summer afternoon, on June 23, 1992, a 10-wheel flatbed truck veered off the road and killed Andolsek. He was hit from behind and died shortly after being taken to the hospital.

It was a stunning turn of events for the Lions who had lost guard Mike Utley seven months earlier when he was paralyzed after an on-field hit.

Ron Hughes, the Lions personnel director, said he couldn't believe how many people had asked him how the Lions were going to replace Eric. "I don't think we'll ever replace him for the simple reason I don't think people realize how good that kid was. He was unbelievable," Hughes told reporters.

Not only was Andolsek emerging as one of the NFL's top guards, but the leadership qualities of the four-year veteran were rare.

His teammates' respect for him was exhibited one final time when many of them made the trip to St. John's Catholic Church in Thibodaux for Andolsek's funeral mass. Lions attending included Spielman, Lomas Brown, Mark Spindler, and Rodney Peete. Coach Wayne Fontes was also in attendance.

Every spot in the 450-seat chapel was taken, according to newspaper reports.

Peete said he still couldn't believe his teammate was gone. He said he played his answering machine message back five times to make sure he heard it correctly.

Andolsek's size (6'2", 286 pounds) led to his nicknames—Table and Biggie.

Andolsek was laid to rest in a marble crypt in the town of 15,000. He was 25.

He left behind his wife, Cheryl, along with many saddened Lions fans.

Andolsek, who played at Louisiana State, had been a fifth-round pick (111th overall) by the Lions in the 1988 draft. At LSU, where he was a captain in 1986 and 1987, he played both offense and defense at the Sugar Bowl against Nebraska on January 1, 1985, when injuries had depleted LSU's defensive line.

He became a starter in his second season, blocking for Barry Sanders.

In 1991 he helped lead the Lions to a 12–4 record and the NFC Championship Game. It was his final game. He was named to *USA Today*'s All-Pro team that year. In the season following his death, the Lions finished 5–11.

When the investigation was complete, it was ruled that neither drinking nor drugs played a role in the fatal accident. There also were no mechanical difficulties with the truck. At first it was thought that perhaps the driver had dozed off, but he later admitted he had been distracted. He was charged with negligent homicide and failure to maintain control of his truck.

Andolsek will not be forgotten.

The Lions have named their outstanding offensive lineman award after him. His number (55) has been retired by Thibodaux High School. Also, LSU has named its outstanding senior in spring practice the Eric Andolsek Award.

"Here was a guy making great money in the NFL; he could have played 10 more years, and he came back to Thibodaux," former LSU linebacker Shawn Burks told *The Morning Advocate* the day Andolsek died. "He built his own house, he moved right next to his mom and dad, and he still had the same friends from high school, which says everything about the guy right there.... He'll be missed."

He still is.

87 Morton's Impact

You can take a young man out of California, but you can't take the California out of a young man. That was wide receiver Johnnie Morton, the Lions first-round draft pick in 1994 from the University of Southern California. He made his mark in eight seasons with the Lions until Matt Millen tossed him aside after the 2001 season. We'll get back to that.

Morton was a health nut before it was cool. He'd offer to share his bags of whole-wheat pretzels with his teammates and media, but he had few takers after it was discovered the pretzels tasted like sawdust. Ironically, he was also known for his homemade peach cobbler.

Morton kept in excellent shape. He went seven straight seasons in Detroit without missing a game. His body-fat level was near non-existent.

As a rookie in 1994, Morton had some tough competition to get on the field with teammates like Herman Moore and Brett Perriman. In 1995, one of the Lions' most explosive offensive seasons ever, Morton was the featured slot receiver and a kickoff/punt returner.

Morton's best season statistically came in 1999 when he had 80 receptions for 1,129 yards on a team that surprisingly made the playoffs after getting the news just before training camp that Barry Sanders had retired.

The Tiramisu Cheesecake

In the early 1990s, wide receiver Johnnie Morton was a bit of a health-conscious nut. He would brag about his low body-fat count.

So it was odd one Saturday to have the following interaction with him at a mall in suburban Indianapolis the day before a game. He saw me wandering around, and I mentioned I would be making a stop at The Cheesecake Factory. Without hesitation, he told me to order the tiramisu cheesecake. He told me I wouldn't be disappointed. I wasn't. It still ranks as one of my top five desserts ever—and I've tried many of them.

How Mr. Low Body-Fat could lead someone to a dessert loaded with fat was beyond me. Just glad I took the advice. Years later, I still visit that mall when I'm in Indianapolis and I still order that same scrumptious slice of high-fat heaven.

In the 1995 Thanksgiving shootout win over Minnesota, Morton was one of three wide receivers to surpass the 100-yard mark that day. He had 102 yards, Brett Perriman had 153 yards, and Herman Moore had 127 yards. That day Sanders rushed for 138 yards, and Scott Mitchell passed for 410.

Morton was never one to keep quiet.

He loved the limelight—perhaps it was the California in him.

In 2001 when the Lions started the season 0–12, NBC's Jay Leno made frequent jokes about the Lions. So after their first win, Morton sent the message, "Jay Leno can kiss my ass." Morton was later invited to the show, and Leno kissed a donkey.

Matt Millen didn't re-sign Morton after the 2001 season. Instead, Morton was signed by the Kansas City Chiefs and played three seasons there (2002–05). That's where he broke out his famous "worm" touchdown dance. (See YouTube.)

There was no love lost between Millen and Morton.

In December 2003, following a Lions' 45–17 loss at the Kansas City Chiefs, Millen was trying to congratulate some of the Chiefs players near the Chiefs locker room when he confronted Morton who had nothing to say to him. Then when he walked by Morton, Millen said, "Hey Johnnie," and was ignored. Then Millen said something like, "nice talking to you" and Morton told him to kiss his ass.

Then, by all reports, Millen said, "You faggot! Yeah, you heard me, faggot." The mean-spirited comment was heard by a Chiefs media relations staff member and a Kansas City columnist. Millen later apologized for the incident that Morton called demeaning and bigoted.

Morton, whose brother Chad was a running back at USC and played on four NFL teams, finished his NFL career by playing one season (1995) with the San Francisco 49ers.

He attempted a career in Mixed Martial Arts but was knocked out in 38 seconds in his one bout on June 2, 2007.

It takes all kinds of characters to create any successful NFL team. Morton was one of those guys.

He and Herman Moore had lockers next to each other and routinely entertained the gathered media.

Morton wasn't the most prolific wide receiver with the Lions, but he was a critical part of the 1995 team.

88 Porcher, A Community Man

A defensive end who played with passion, fire, and intensity, Robert Porcher ended his career with dignity. After 12 seasons with the Lions, including three trips to the Pro Bowl, Porcher was flanked by Matt Millen and Steve Mariucci at the press conference on November 1, 2004, for his farewell.

It was his way of saying good-bye and, by all accounts, it was emotional.

Shaun Rogers, the new leader of the defensive line, was sitting in the front row fighting back tears. With Porcher, the defensive line was the strength of the team. Rogers knew he had big cleats to fill.

Porcher had planned to play in the 2004 season, but there were eight healthy defensive linemen in front of him on the depth chart. So in October he had asked Millen for his release. He had no desire to go to a different NFL team after all those years in Detroit.

Porcher didn't want his teammates to think that he was quitting on them. It was just his time to step away from the game after being a fixture on the Lions' defensive line for 12 years.

He was honored at the final home game of the 2004 season when he served as honorary captain amid loud cheers from the

Lions' faithful. Porcher was always a fan favorite because they knew he would get the job done.

Porcher made his mark in the record books and in the city of Detroit, as well.

He still holds the franchise record for career sacks with 95.5. He's in fourth place for sacks in a season (15) behind Al "Bubba" Baker, who holds first through third (23, 18, 16). Porcher is tied for eighth for most sacks in one game (3.5). He's tied for third for number of games played (187). Wait, there's more. He led the team in sacks in eight seasons, and he became the first Lion to record double-digit sacks in four consecutive years (1996–99). He played in 24 career games where he had more than one sack.

Porcher was drafted in the first round in 1992 out of South Carolina State and then made Detroit his home.

In 2003 he was given the Ed Block Memorial Courage Award, which recognizes men of courage, and he was a finalist for the NFL's Walter Payton Man of the Year Award.

There's a reason the Lions' annual man of the year award is named The Robert Porcher Man of the Year honor.

Porcher was active in the community. His foundation for cancer research and relief raised funds for the University of Michigan Comprehensive Cancer Center.

Porcher left the game with no regrets, and he was the same strong pass-rush specialist near the end of his career. In the strongest stretch of his career, 1996–2001, he had 68 sacks and was named to the Pro Bowl three times (1997, 1999, 2001).

He was honored that he had played his entire career with the team that drafted him. Not only that—he had played for five head coaches and nine defensive coordinators.

After retirement, Porcher got into the restaurant business in Detroit. As vice president of the Southern Hospitality Restaurant Group, he was named to the 40 Under 40 list by *Crain's Detroit Business* in 2006.

89 Visit Training Camp, Learn New Words

In recent years, the Lions have started a training-camp tradition where young children are picked from the crowd to walk the players onto the field and carry their helmets.

The players seem to enjoy it, chatting with the kids, asking about their names and interests. Many of the kids are wearing Lions jerseys. Some of them try on the helmets, which are quite heavy. Some of them are almost too stunned to say a word, while others can't shut up.

Kids, who can be brutally honest, aren't afraid to say that Calvin Johnson or Matthew Stafford is their favorite player, even if they're walking out with Nate Burleson or Shaun Hill.

It's all part of the fun in Allen Park, Michigan. The players seem to realize they're part of a special moment and are up for it.

Parents can get photos of their kids with the players. That's all part of the fun, too.

Lions training camp is free, entertaining, and perhaps the best chance for fans to see their favorite players up close. Unless you've got the best seats in the house at Ford Field, you won't get any closer.

The Lions open most of their training-camp sessions to the general public on a first-come, first-serve basis. A few crazies line up in the early morning hours, to be the first ones through the gate. No one remembers turning fans away.

Every day there's an autograph table where four players will sit after practice and sign away while chatting with fans. All the players take turns signing, which means maybe you won't get a marquee player. But maybe you'll get someone who won't be unknown for long.

It's often hot and steamy, but for someone who's never been to a practice it can be a bit of an eye opener.

A big hit now and then and an occasional rumble are all part of training camp on a daily basis.

If you're wondering who's lining up where and which rookie is standing out at camp, this is the place to be. Of course rookies can be up and down, and they may amaze fans more than they do coaches, but it's all part of the camp fun that leads to the cut-down to the 53-man roster.

Fantasy geeks, and I mean that in the nicest way, can get a look at who might be a good pickup that no one else knows about.

Even though you can get close, binoculars would be a good bet. The players work out on side-by-side fields, and the far field can provide more challenges to get a good view.

The Lions welcome fans and don't charge for entrance or for parking. The practice facility, which is right off the Southfield expressway, is easy to find.

Off to Camp

Since the Lions started having training camps in 1934 they have been held in 10 different locations. It started at Cranbrook, a private school in Bloomfield Hills, and stayed there through 1941. Then they moved on to Charlevoix in 1942, West Shore Golf Club in Grosse Ile in 1943 and 1944, Assumption College in Windsor 1945, Alma College 1946–48, Michigan State Normal College in Ypsilanti 1949–56, back to Cranbrook from 1957–74, Oakland University from 1975–89, Pontiac Silverdome from 1990–96, Saginaw Valley State University from 1997–2001 and at the Lions practice facility from 2002 to the present.

The question comes up every summer on whether the Lions will take training camp on the road again. Every summer there are rumors it will be moved to a college campus somewhere in Michgian. The rumors are just that. Although a change in scenery is always a possibility.

For those enjoying stay-cations, it's easily something that you could build a day around. If you're really into it, you could also visit the Henry Ford Museum and Greenfield Village a stone's throw away.

The Lions provide bleacher seats, rosters, and they have a souvenir trailer along with a snack bar.

They provide the basic necessities, including Porta-Johns. (Note: if you see a player heading to the bushes, it's because there are no outdoor facilities for the players.)

It's a great family opportunity.

Your children may even learn some words they've never heard unless they have a parent who swears like an NFL player, working out in the heat and humidity for the umpteenth straight day.

That's part of the fun, too.

The Lions aren't crazy. Training camp is a great way to get fans interested. And quite often interested fans become paying fans.

90 First Impressions

When the Lions bring in potential free agents and/or draft picks, their first impression of the Detroit Lions is the practice facility in Allen Park. It's about a 10-minute drive from the airport, so it's the first stop on the tour. It doesn't hurt that it's a glistening, state-of-the-art facility.

When the Lions were losing for all those years, it wasn't easy to attract quality free agents. It's not like a great practice facility can seal the deal, but it certainly is a bonus.

When the Lions decided to make the move from the Pontiac Silverdome and build Ford Field in Detroit, they decided to build

Running back Allen Irvin carries the ball through a drill during training camp on Sunday, August 2, 2009, in Allen Park, Michigan. (AP Photo/Duane Burleson)

a new training and practice facility. The $35.5 million headquarters and training facility is built on 22.7 acres just west of Detroit and down the street from the Ford World Headquarters in Dearborn. It's just off the Southfield Freeway and is easy to get to from anywhere in metro Detroit.

It sits on the edge of a industrial park alongside a marsh area. It's so close to Henry Ford Museum and Greenfield Village that you can hear the train whistles from the outdoor fields.

The complex of 253,000 square feet includes a full indoor practice field (220' wide by 440' long), two outdoor practice fields, a state-of-the art weight and training room, a massive locker room, a hydrotherapy room, a spacious equipment room, a cafeteria, meeting rooms for each position, a player lounge, a 103-person auditorium for full team meetings and large press conferences, a

Packing Up For Camp

When Bobby Ross became coach, he wanted to get the team away for training camp. He wanted them to concentrate solely on football for the first few weeks. The solution was to hold camp on the campus of Saginaw Valley State University, about a 90-mile drive north on I-75 from the Silverdome.

The players stayed in dorms and buzzed around campus in golf carts. It was all football all the time, with no family issues and not much free time. Although one night as a surprise treat, Ross had the team bussed to a local cinema for a showing of *There's Something About Mary*.

Camp was open to the fans, and they flocked in. Not only was everything free, but the Saginaw Valley State campus was right off I-75 and many fans would stop on the way up north for a vacation or on the way home.

There were inflatables for the kids and concessions—but mostly there was football. It was a good deal all around. The players loved the applause they'd receive for a big play now and then. It kept them going during those hot, humid Michigan summer days.

studio, a library and archive room with newspaper clips that go back to the 1930s, a media room, and offices for all personnel.

The Lions work out at the facility in the off-season. Also it's where they practice daily throughout the season. The weekly coach's press conferences on Mondays are held in the television studio.

On NFL draft weekend, it's where all the decisions are made. All the executive offices are at this facility rather than Ford Field.

The indoor practice field has a height of 110'. A balcony along one side allows the media and occasional special guests to watch practice. Like Ford Field, it features field turf.

All of that and it's a certified green building, too.

It was built with renewable and recyclable products, including bamboo floors in the lobby and lights that automatically turn on as the room is entered.

The outdoor fields, where training camp is held, are spacious enough that camp practices can be open to the public. Also with two and a half fields side by side, the Lions can rotate from one field to another to keep the grass fresh and not allow it to get worn down, especially during training camp. Although not a key feature, back beyond the storage shed behind the outdoor fields there is a putting green.

Ground was broken for the facility on August 7, 2000, and it was completed 19 months later. The grand opening was April 22, 2002, just in time for the NFL draft.

The facility also honors two special men who had connections with the Lions and died young. The indoor practice area is named Ricky Sandoval Field. Sandoval was the Lions' director of security who lost a courageous three-year battle with pancreatic cancer on July 2, 2009. He was 49.

The media workrooms on the first floor are named for Tom Kowalski, a longtime Lions beat writer who died of heart issues in August 2011.

91 From Player to Player Personnel

For Sheldon White the biggest difference in taking the huge step from NFL player to management is understanding how much more is involved in the daily operations. It was an eye opener for White, who was a defensive back with the Lions from 1990–92.

He's not the only former Lion in management. Hall of Famer Charlie Sanders has stayed around and is now assistant director of pro personnel. Assistant special teams coach Bradford Banta is a former Lions long snapper. In years past, Hall of Fame linebacker Joe Schmidt moved into the head coaching position after just one year as an assistant.

There's clearly been an effort for the Lions to stay connected with alumni in general, particularly the guys who live locally.

"I think that's important, and I think when you can involve those guys in the organization it helps everybody—it helps the organization and it helps those guys," team president Tom Lewand said.

"Within that group of guys, there are people who have particularly useful skills that match up with needs that we have. Sheldon is a very talented executive and he's talented, hard working, very organized, very diligent, he brought that to the table as an entry-level scout in the late '90s when Ron Hughes hired him," Lewand said. "Those characteristics propelled him into the pro personnel director role right when Kevin Colbert left [for the Steelers] and the key role he's in now."

When White retired in 1993, he knew he wanted to stay involved in football with a goal of getting back to the NFL. Only this time he would be wearing a suit instead of a uniform.

Immediately after hanging up his cleats, White took a job at Miami of Ohio, his alma mater, coaching wide receivers. He rejoined the Lions in 1997 as a BLESTO scout and has worked his way up to vice president of pro personnel.

With the perspective of a former player, White knows the type of person he's looking for to join the Lions. It's not someone who just wants to live off the big salary.

White and the Lions look for guys who love to play the game. Of course, they have to have talent and all that goes with it. But it's a love of the game that can ultimately bring success.

92 Pro Football Hall of Fame

The Pro Football Hall of Fame is not just a building. It's inspiration, it's history, it's a tribute to the game of football, and one of its members, Charlie Sanders, can be seen at the Lions practice facility daily.

In August 2011 the Lions were taking a bus south to Cleveland for a preseason game, and coach Jim Schwartz thought it presented a perfect opportunity for a stop at the Hall of Fame. On the visit, the current Lions players saw that less than 300 players were special enough for the honor. It kind of shed a new light on Sanders, who is the Lions assistant director of pro personnel.

"I think guys walk through there and maybe they're younger and don't have an appreciation for the game as much or they don't have an appreciation for the Hall of Fame per se. Most of these guys have been or will be put into the high school halls of fames or college halls of fame, but when you realize there's only 300-plus guys in there and how much those men in that hall have made this

Who's Next for Canton?

Will it be a long wait before the next member of the Lions is inducted into the Hall of Fame? It might all depend on how long kicker Jason Hanson continues to play. After 2011, he still had two years left on his contract.

Hanson has shattered Lions kicking records, along with NFL records. He seems a lock to be a Pro Football Hall of Famer.

Roger Brown, a defensive lineman from 1960–66 with Detroit, could still get the call. Perhaps he's been the most overlooked Lion who deserves a call from the Hall.

game what it is today," Lions president Tom Lewand said. "Then you realize one of them is here everyday. And when you're Brandon Pettigrew and you realize one of the guys who redefined the [tight end] position is right down the hall, that gives you a different lens to look through. I think a much different appreciation for it."

The visit was a hit with the players, and many didn't want to leave.

"They were in different areas looking at the old uniforms, the old shoes, the main hall with the busts. Some of the modern stuff, Jason Hanson's shoes were in there for a record he'd set for 50-yard field goals, Stafford's jersey was in there that was cut off from the Cleveland game," Lewand said, referring to the game after Stafford was literally down on the sideline with a shoulder injury, forced his way back into the game, and engineered a win.

"[The Hall] provides a different perspective they don't always get when they come into this building every day. Especially those guys who are high draft choices, who are doted upon all through their college experience, who are doted on up until draft day. They're doted on until the time they walk into this building," Lewand said. "To step back, a lot of them don't have that perspective."

For a few years, Charlie Sanders would take rookies down to the Hall of Fame for a tour each year. The league recognizes the importance of players honoring the past, and so do the Lions.

"It does provide a sense of context, which I think is important, and guys can't lose sight of that fact," Lewand said. "And whether it's a guy who wants to have an appreciation for where the game has come from, or whether it's a guy who renews his resolve to get his own bust in there. I think it really does put it in perspective."

Seventeen other former Lions have been enshrined in the Pro Football Hall of Fame.

Along with Charlie Sanders, the other former Lions who are enshrined in the Hall of Fame include Barry Sanders, Lem Barney, Dick LeBeau, Lou Creekmur, Joe Schmidt, Earl "Dutch" Clark, Dick "Night Train" Lane, Bobby Layne, Yale Lary, Jack Christiansen, Bill Dudley, Frank Gatski, John Henry Johnson, Ollie Matson, Hugh McElhenny, Doak Walker, and Alex Wojciechowicz.

The Pro Football Hall of Fame in Canton, Ohio, is just a little more than 200 miles from Detroit. Give yourself plenty of time to soak in all the history.

93 The Handshake

Emotions run high on the field before, during, and after any NFL game. It's not just the players who occasionally lose control.

After San Francisco snapped the Lions' five-game win streak on October 16, 2011, with a 25–19 win, 49ers coach Jim Harbaugh shook Jim Schwartz's hand aggressively, then slapped him on the back, nearly pushing him off balance.

The exchange set off a chain of events that was the talk of Detroit and the NFL for weeks to come. Two coaches going at it? Not an everyday NFL sideshow.

No doubt Harbaugh was the instigator, the rookie head coach who had just beaten a talented undefeated Lions team on their home turf.

Schwartz said he wasn't expecting the obscenity that followed. That's when the Lions coach, with a look on his face that was downright scary, started chasing Harbaugh into the tunnel before he was grabbed by Lions security director Elton Moore.

In hindsight, it's easy to say Schwartz could have taken the high road and walked away. Have you met the guy? He's a fireball of emotion and intensity, fueled by the competitiveness and the desire to win.

"We're an emotional team, and we go as our head coach goes, we're going to continue to approach the game with passion," wide

San Francisco 49ers head coach Jim Harbaugh (left) and Detroit Lions head coach Jim Schwartz (right) shout at each other after a game in Detroit on Sunday, October 16, 2011. The 49ers won 25–19. (AP Photo/Rick Osentoski)

receiver Nate Burleson said. "With how we've been playing, it's a direct reflection of how Jim is. That's been pretty good for us so far."

Exactly.

The Sunday postgame brouhaha was a heat-of-the-moment situation, it was Schwartz's home field where he's brought legitimacy back to a long-suffering franchise and its fans.

Walk away? Get serious.

Schwartz didn't walk away from the issue on Monday, either. A reporter opened the door for an apology and the coach slammed it shut by saying, "It's a regrettable situation, I think the fact that it detracted from what happened in the game, I think I'll just leave it right there."

He said that repeatedly on Monday—that it was a shame the skirmish overshadowed one of the better NFL games played on Sunday.

The NFL announced they would not fine either coach because there was no fighting involved. Schwartz said he had talked to the league on Monday and "just told them what happened."

Sports Illustrated's Peter King suggested if head coaches still wore suits on the sideline, this wouldn't have happened. Not so sure about that. The emotions of Harbaugh and Schwartz could not be contained by expensive designer suits.

The two have a past but not much of one. When Harbaugh was a quarterback for the Baltimore Ravens, Schwartz was a lowly defensive quality control coach. "I mean, I haven't exactly stayed in touch," Schwartz said.

But according to a *Philadelphia Inquirer* article, the two had dinner with John Harbaugh, the Ravens coach, and Jim's brother, and a bigger group at the owners' meetings in March.

"We were having dinner the other night, and Jim Schwartz told [Jim Harbaugh] basically there's no way you're going to be able to get it done [if the lockout lasts into the summer]," John Harbaugh said to the *Inquirer*. "He told him there's no way you're going to

The Non-Handshake

While the handshake, backslap, and whiplash between Lions coach Jim Schwartz and 49ers coach Jim Harbaugh was the talk of the town, there was another handshake incident in 2011.

Lions general manager Martin Mayhew blew off a handshake with Kansas City Chiefs general manager Scott Pioli at the Ford Field elevators following the Lions' win over the Chiefs on September 18. The Chiefs had charged the Lions with tampering in 2010, so there was no love lost.

"As an organization we haven't really mastered that whole postgame handshake thing," Mayhew said. "We're still working on that. We'll get that right next year.... Maybe we'll do some drills on that," he added.

be able to accomplish what you need to accomplish in two weeks if this thing lasts a while. Jim just kind of bit his tongue, which is what you've got to do in this situation. Because there's nothing you can do about it."

The only thing Jim Harbaugh could do was mark his calendar for October 16, go to Ford Field, and beat the Lions. He did all three. Perhaps the handshake and slap on the back were just the exclamation point. Perhaps that dinner conversation had nothing to do with it. Schwartz and Harbaugh are driven men and assets to the NFL. Winning is everything, and losing is painful.

"I've shaken hands, I don't know, 40–50 times over the last two and a half years or so, never had anything come up, obviously something did," Schwartz said. "I'll just revert back to what I said [Sunday] and leave it there.

"It is what it is, it happened, it was very regrettable, and it's something that there's nothing going forward between us personally or the two teams."

Forget about it? Get serious.

94 Celebrate in Greektown

If you can't have fun in Greektown, perhaps you should check your pulse.

Within walking distance from Ford Field, Greektown is a go-to destination for postgame celebrations or to drown your sorrows in ouzo.

If you hear out of towners proclaim downtown Detroit dead, you know they've never been to Greektown, which is thriving since the Greektown Casino arrived in 2000.

It's a popular restaurant and entertainment district, a desirable destination for many headed to downtown Detroit. The more well-known restaurants include the Golden Fleece, Laikon Cafe, Cyprus Taverna, Pegasus Taverna, and Pizza Papalis. It might be the only location in Detroit where you'll hear "Oompah" when your saganaki—a cheese appetizer grilled in brandy and set on fire—is brought to your table.

It's hard to forget you're in Greektown because Greek music is played on Monroe Avenue throughout the day.

Greektown also has a stop on the Detroit People Mover, so if you're in another part of the city, you can easily make it to Greektown. Or you can park in Greektown and make your way to Joe Louis Arena or the Cobo Center on the People Mover. To get to Ford Field, you can hoof it or take a cab.

One of the landmarks of Greektown is Old St. Mary's, the third oldest Roman Catholic church in Detroit. It was first built on its present site in 1841 as a parish of German Catholic immigrants. But the present church built in 1884 is styled in Victorian Gothic. It's a masterpiece containing polished columns that are made of solid granite. The ceiling and the stained glass windows could take your breath away. It's truly a Detroit treasure.

Greektown is a historic area listed on the National Register of Historic Places in 1982. It is located just northeast of the downtown center along Monroe Avenue between Brush and St. Antoine streets. It's between the Renaissance Center and Ford Field and Comerica Park.

It wasn't always Greektown. The area was first settled in the 1830s by German immigrants and was primarily a residential neighborhood. In the early 20th century, many Germans moved to neighborhoods further from downtown. That's when Greek immigrants moved in led by Theodore Gerasimos, the first documented Greek immigrant in Detroit. It wasn't always a thriving area, and redevelopment in the 1960s led to the neighborhood becoming more commercialized. Greek leaders didn't want to lose the ethnic feel of the area and worked with the mayor's office to make improvements. The first Greek festival was held in 1966 and held for several years until it just got too large.

When you talk about the flavor of Detroit, Greektown has to be in the conversation—and not just for its restaurants.

95 Working the Line

For nine straight seasons, from 1987–95, Kevin Glover and Lomas Brown anchored the Lions' offensive line. That's a long time for a pair of Pro Bowl–caliber linemen to work almost side by side. (There was usually at least one body between them.)

For several of those seasons, they blocked for a certain running back named Barry Sanders, one of the best all-time rushers. Sanders

*Center Kevin Glover (53) in action during the Lions 38–6 victory over the
Dallas Cowboys in the 1991 NFC Divisional Playoff Game on January 5,
1992, at the Pontiac Silverdome in Pontiac Michigan.* (AP Photo/NFL Photos)

won three rushing titles when the pair was on the offensive line
blocking for him (1990 and 1994) and won two others in 1996
and 1997.

The two were instrumental in the Lions' NFC Central
Division titles in 1991 and 1993 and playoff berths in 1994, 1995,
and 1997. They were on the 1991 team that was the last Lions team
to win a playoff game.

Brown was drafted in 1985 out of the University of Florida in
the first round (sixth overall). As a rookie he started at left tackle, and
it was a position he held for the Lions for 11 seasons through 1995.
Brown started all but one of the 164 games he played for the Lions.

For seven consecutive seasons (1990–96), Brown was named to the Pro Bowl, and he was first team All-Pro in 1991, 1992, and 1995.

He finished his 18-year NFL career on top when he won a Super Bowl ring with the Tampa Bay Buccaneers in 2002. After his 11 seasons with the Lions, Brown played for the Arizona Cardinals (1996–98), the Cleveland Browns (1999), the New York Giants

Offensive tackle Lomas Brown (75) looks to block Rams defensive tackle Shawn Miller (98) in a 14–24 Detroit Lions preseason loss to the Los Angeles Rams on September 9, 1989, at Anaheim Stadium in Anaheim, California. (AP Photo/ NFL Photos)

(2000–01), and Tampa Bay (2002). He started in 251 of the 263 NFL games he played in.

Brown and Glover had the honor of blocking for Sanders who always showed appreciation for the line's ability to help him break free. The offensive line was also recognized for its pass protection. In 1995, the Lions, behind quarterback Scott Mitchell, set passing records that stood until Matthew Stafford and the Lions' offense came along in the 2011 season.

Glover was drafted in the same draft as Brown but in the second round out of Maryland. Unlike Brown he didn't start right away, which is not at all uncommon for offensive linemen. When Glover started in the 1987 season, it was at right guard. In 1988, he moved to left guard and moved to center in 1989 where he played until the Lions let him go after the 1997 season.

Glover knew Lions coach Bobby Ross well because he had played for him for three seasons at Maryland.

Glover, who played 13 seasons for the Lions, went to three straight Pro Bowls from 1995–97. Glover and Barry Sanders had become close friends through the years. Sanders had criticized the Lions' front office for releasing Glover after the 1997 season for salary cap reasons.

When the Lions let him go, Glover played two more seasons for the Seattle Seahawks.

96 Detroit Lions Charities

The Lions as a team are committed to the community, but they couldn't be as successful without help from the players.

A good example was the 2011 Detroit Lions Invitational golf tournament, one of the team's main fund-raisers each year. For several years it's been held at the exclusive TPC of Michigan in Dearborn, just down the street from the Lions practice facility.

Everything was a little different in June 2011 due to the NFL lockout. The players couldn't have contact with the coaches and couldn't enter the practice facility, but there was a provision that allowed players to attend charity events as long as they didn't talk shop with the coaches.

In other words, the players really were under no obligation to show up.

But to support the Detroit Lions Charities, many of them were there, including Matthew Stafford, Drew Stanton, Dominic Raiola, and Jeff Backus. Nate Burleson, Nick Fairley, and Shaun Hill didn't play golf but attended to lend their support.

"We're just here to raise some money for Detroit Lions Charities, have a little fun, and enjoy the weather, no other reason," Jim Schwartz said that day. "On the back nine you're not going

There Is Crying In Football

Tim Pendell left quite a legacy with the Lions when he retired early in 2011. In his 26 years with the team, Pendell was instrumental in creating the Detroit Lions Charities that was launched in 1990 to assist all age groups in a diverse range of needs and programs in Michigan.

One of his fondest memories from his years with the Lions came on Thanksgiving in 1989, which happened to be the 20th anniversary for him and his wife, Diann.

Since the Lions play every Thanksgiving, Pendell was at work at the Silverdome in a game against the Cleveland Browns. It was Barry Sanders' rookie year. The Lions had 13 players out of the game with injuries. They had no business beating the Browns, but they did, 13–10.

"I can remember, I don't mind saying tears were coming down my face. It was 1989. I'd been sick. In 1988, Diann had been sick and at the end of the year we won that big Thanskgiving Day game. We weren't having a particularly good season, but we rose to the occasion with a bunch of guys who worked their tails off," Pendell said.

to see guys doing 7-on-7s, sprinting down the fairways, or swimming in the ponds, maybe we could do some sand work in the bunkers.... There's a time and place for everything. Now's the time to raise money for charity."

The team commitment to the community starts at the top and runs throughout the organization, which created Detroit Lions Charities 20 years ago. In the 2009–10 season, grants were awarded totaling $345,829.13. In the history of the organization, more than $5.6 million has been awarded.

Grants are awarded to all age groups in a diverse range of needs in Michigan but more emphasis is placed on programs for the children and youth of Detroit.

A prime example is the annual grant of about $60,000 to the Think Detroit PAL Football League, which involves 3,200 youngsters each season in one of the nation's largest tackle football leagues. Most grants are smaller in value, but that allows the charity to spread the wealth. In March 2010, they issued 88 grants that totaled $345,829.13.

Any organization can apply for grant money by going to the Detroit Lions website and determining if their group meets the standards.

97 Coney Wars

Chicago has pizza, Philadelphia has cheese steak, and Detroit has Coney Islands.

It's a Motor City phenomena. Visitors don't understand the Coney Island phenomena until they chow down on one or two. Or three.

The basic recipe for a Coney Island involves seasoned ground beef covering a Coney hot dog topped with chili, mustard, and onions, served in a steamed bun. The quality of the hot dogs, usually with natural casings, can vary as well as the flavor of the chili that is beanless.

It's not just the dogs, the restaurants also offer loose hamburger sandwiches, and there's always a special with dogs and loose hamburger combined. It's a gastronomic delight.

The only thing that separates Coney lovers is which place they prefer. In downtown Detroit the two standards are American and Lafayette, located nearly side by side on Lafayette Street. American is at 114 W. Lafayette, with Lafayette at 118 W. Lafayette.

Coney lovers are usually intensely loyal to one or the other. The debate often goes back for generations.

For a historical perspective, American is the oldest and has been family owned and operated since 1917. It was opened by Gust Keros who immigrated to Detroit from Greece in 1910 and opened American Coney Island in 1929 where he sold nickel dogs.

He was so successful he brought his brother William over from Greece and trained him. When the storefront next door became available, William started Lafayette Coney Island. Third-generation family members still run both locales, which have remained side by side for more than 70 years.

Both are open 24 hours a day, seven days a week. Amidst Detroit's economic hard times, a Coney Island can always be had. They're not a nickel any more, but they are reasonable at a little more than $2.

American boasts high-quality, specially-seasoned, natural-skin-casing hot dog from Dearborn Sausage and their own Keros family secret recipe Coney Island Chili Sauce developed decades ago. Add to that a topping of fine mustard and sweet chopped onions that is the final touch to the distinctive overall taste and flavor.

I asked some friends on Facebook to tell me their preference. In a totally unscientific survey, Lafayette won by a landslide.

According to Marylynn Hewitt, "Love the atmosphere with the guys in white aprons and caps, yelling the orders in verbal shorthand, their extra crispy fries are the best, and even the thick plates and coffee mugs match the decor of an old diner. All the windows offer the landscape of the diversity that makes up downtown Detroit."

Bob Gritzinger said, "Lafayette for the inscrutable waitstaff, the great Coney's and the, shall we say, 'scenic' facilities in the basement."

Mike O'Hara said, "Lafayette. Plus the banana cream pie—after closing time. Intestinal Stridex—soaking up the alcohol for the ride home."

Suburbanites make their way to both downtown locations. There are also a few chains, such as National, that have been around since 1965. They can be found all through the suburbs.

Let's just say this, if you're in Detroit and hankering for a Coney, you can find one without much trouble. You just have to understand your taste preference.

98 History at the Lions' Expense

On November 8, 1970, kicker Tom Dempsey of the New Orleans Saints made history. The Lions were his victims. With 2 seconds remaining in the game and the Saints down 17–16, Saints holder Joe Scarpati knelt at his own 37-yard line at Tulane Stadium in New Orleans after taking a good snap from Jackie Burkett. At the time the goal posts were on the goal lines. (They moved to the end lines in 1974.)

Dempsey took two and a half steps into it, and the ball sailed with a brisk tailwind and made it through the lower right corner of the goal posts.

The 63-yard field goal set a record, shattering the previous mark of 56 yards. It was the longest field goal in 51 years of professional football and, as a bonus, won the game for New Orleans. It was one of just two wins that season for the Saints.

"It's like winning the Masters with a 390-yard hole-in-one on the last shot," Lions coach Joe Schmidt said.

Dempsey was so far back he didn't see the ball clear the crossbar. It made it with 2' left to spare. Earlier in the game he had a 24-yarder deflected by the Lions. Afterward Lions quarterback Greg Landry took the blame.

He had conducted the "heroic" drive that led to the 18-yard field goal by Errol Mann that had given the Lions the 17–16 lead with 11 seconds remaining. When it was over, Landry realized he should have run down the clock more. He just didn't conceive that the Saints would attempt a 63-yard field goal.

After the Lions' field goal with 11 seconds remaining, they kicked off to the Saints, who returned it to their own 28-yard line. Then quarterback Bill Kilmer found Al Dodd with a sideline pass to the 45 for a 17-yard gain.

Two seconds were left on the clock, and that was plenty for Tom Dempsey who became a folk hero of sorts. Dempsey was born without toes on his right foot. He was fit with a special shoe that was approved by the NFL and kicked with that right foot. He was also born with no fingers on his right hand.

Three weeks earlier Mann had predicted that someone would kick a 60-yard field goal. But on that day Mann said he didn't expect Dempsey would make it after watching him in practice and during his other kicks in the game. "I didn't think he'd get one 63 yards," Mann told reporters.

No one did.

Not only did it shock the Lions, it dropped their record to 5–3. They lost again the next week but won five straight to end the season with a 10–4 record, finishing second in the NFC Central. They lost at Dallas 5–0 in the playoff game.

The 63-yard field goal record still stood in 2011, although it had been equaled twice.

The first was on October 25, 1998, by Jason Elam of the Denver Broncos against the Jacksonville Jaguars at Mile High Stadium in Denver. The second occurred on September 12, 2011, by Sebastian Janikowski of the Oakland Raiders against the Denver Broncos at Sports Authority Field at Mile High in Denver. Notice both were kicked in the thin air at Denver.

Perhaps there should be an asterisk next to Dempsey's field goal.

There was a little belly-aching that he had an unfair advantage with more flat surface on his shoes. Perhaps that's why, in 1977, the NFL added a rule that's known as the Tom Dempsey Rule. It says, "Any shoe that is worn by a player with an artificial limb on his kicking leg must have a kicking surface that conforms to that of a normal kicking shoe."

99 Bears-Lions Rivalry

It's not just the length of time that has created the rivalry between the Lions and the Chicago Bears, it's the intensity.

Starting in 1930, the two legendary franchises have faced each other at least twice per season (except in 1987 the lockout-shortened season). They've met 164 times, which makes the Bears the most common opponent in Lions' history. Detroit has come out on the short end, holding a 65–94–5 record in the series.

Again, it's not the years, it's the physicality and nastiness on the field that create a rival worth writing about. It's still alive if the two games in 2011 were any indication.

The two met on *Monday Night Football* on October 10, which was a huge game for the Lions. The 24–13 win gave them a 5–0 start to the season.

Their win streak was extended to nine, going back to the final four wins last season. Not many Detroit Lions fans were even born the last time the franchise won nine straight games back in the 1953–54 seasons.

With the win, the Lions snapped a six-game losing streak against the Bears. Detroit's last win against the Bears was on October 28, 2007, when the Lions won 16–7 at Soldier Field. This was the fifth Monday night meeting for the Lions and Bears. The Lions are 4–1 in those match-ups.

The Lions sacked Jay Cutler three times—one each for Cliff Avril, Lawrence Jackson, and Willie Young.

The atmosphere was more electric than Ford Field had ever been for a Lions' game. It was so loud that the Bears were whistled for nine false-start penalties. The teams combined for 26 penalties for 198 yards.

But that was nothing compared to a month later when the Bears used their homefield advantage and slammed the Lions 37–13. Detroit's Ndamukong Suh ripped off Jay Cutler's helmet and wasn't penalized. A year before Suh had been fined after he clothes-lined Cutler from behind.

Chicago's D.J. Moore was ejected after a sideline melee that started when Moore leveled quarterback Matthew Stafford at the end of an interception return by Tim Jennings after Stafford took Moore to the ground by the back of his helmet.

Rookie defensive tackle Nick Fairley, possibly following in Suh's footsteps, was called for roughing the passer when he drove Cutler's right shoulder into the turf in the end zone. Bears linebacker Lance Briggs drew a penalty for unnecessary roughness for a hit on Lions wide receiver Calvin Johnson. The Bears take pride in forcing turnovers, and they did it six times in the win. The Lions had only had five turnovers in their previous eight games. Get the picture?

The rivalry has ebbed and flowed throughout the years. With the Lions struggling for so long, it hadn't been the same.

In 2010 and 2011 the Lions showed some growl as they started their turn-around into a team that hopefully will compete hard for years to come.

The rivalry started before the Lions were the Lions. It began back when they were the Portsmouth (Ohio) Spartans. The franchise moved to Detroit in 1934 and won their first championship in 1935. The Lions couldn't have done it except they beat the Bears 14–2 on Thanksgiving on their way to the championship game.

It's been that long and it's still going strong.

It's not just the Bears and Lions when it comes to Chicago-Detroit rivalries. The Red Wings and Blackhawks aren't exactly on friendly terms, either.

100 God Bless YouTube

You Tube is a one-stop site where you can search for your favorite Lions videos from the past and present.

Even though I was at many of Barry Sanders' games at the Silverdome through his Lions career, I'm still amazed when I watch his highlights. There's a great video called "Barry on Barry" where he's watching his highlights and making comments at the same time. He talks about how balance is the key, and he's being humble as usual. On one particularly spectacular run, he said, "For whatever reason I was able to stay up." It was a complete understatement. There's a clip of him running minus a shoe, which he said made it tough to cut. And he sums up his innate ability to get away from, through, and over defenders by saying, "Survivalism is part of the human instinct." Good stuff.

Going back in time, there are historical looks at the Lions championships in 1952, 1953, and 1957. Not the full game, but highlights with that goofy old-time music you usually hear on news reels. It's good stuff, if a little fuzzy.

There's a great video of Chris Spielman going up against a Detroit television reporter who had the odd notion he might be able to stand up to Spielman. It was Don Shane and part of his "Dare Don" television segment.

Spielman blew up. Actually he picked him up (Shane looked so tiny in his uniform and helmet) and dropped him to the ground, not unlike what he might do with any opponent. Kind of crazy, eh? Think an NFL linebacker is going to make a TV guy look good? Well, not Spielman.

Of course you can watch Ndamukong Suh's stomp, but that's so fresh there's not much reason to relive it.

However, the win over Cleveland, engineered by Matthew Stafford in his rookie season, is worth 6:27 of your time. Look up "Matthew Stafford mic'd up Lions vs. Browns." If anyone ever had doubts about Stafford's toughness, they should have been completely erased after that effort.

Here's a great one that you might not remember, depending on your age. It was Billy Sims in a 1983 game against Houston employing a karate kick to get a few more yards. He leapt so high while carrying the ball that instead of stiff-arming a defender, he used his right leg in what looked like a karate kick.

Bobby Layne's official Hall of Fame highlight reel gives a real look into the quarterback and the person with comments from many of his teammates.

Once you start looking around for Lions highlights, it's hard to stop. Don't say I didn't warn you.

Sources

Newspapers
Detroit Free Press
Detroit News
Detroit Times
The Oakland Press
Booth Newspapers
USA Today
Associated Press

Websites
Pro Football Hall of Fame, www.profootballhof.com
Mike Utley, www.mikeutley.org
Detroit Lions, www.detroitlions.com
www.pro-football-reference.com

Books
Plimpton, George. *Paper Lion*, 40th Anniversay edition. (Guilford, CT: The Lyons Press, 2003).
Sanders, Barry, with Mark E. McCormick. *Barry Sanders Now You See Him: His Story in His Own Words*. Clerisy Press, 2005.